Harwood Fundamentals of Pure and Applied Economics

BARRIERS TO ENTRY AND STRATEGIC COMPETITION

FUNDAMENTALS OF PURE AND APPLIED ECONOMICS

INDUSTRIAL ECONOMICS II
In 2 Volumes

I	Barriers to Entry and Strategic Competition	*Geroski et al.*
II	Competition Policy in Europe and North America	*Comanor et al.*

BARRIERS TO ENTRY AND STRATEGIC COMPETITION

PAUL GEROSKI, RICHARD J GILBERT,
AND ALEXIS JACQUEMIN

Routledge
Taylor & Francis Group
LONDON AND NEW YORK

First published in 1990 by
Harwood Academic Publishers GmbH

Reprinted in 2001 by
Routledge
2 Park Square, Milton Park, Abingdon, Oxon, OX14 4RN
711 Third Avenue, New York, NY 10017
Transferred to Digital Printing 2007

Routledge is an imprint of the Taylor & Francis Group
First issued in paperback 2013

The publishers have made every effort to contact authors/copyright holders of the works reprinted in *Harwood Fundamentals of Pure & Applied Economics*. This has not been possible in every case, however, and we would welcome correspondence from those individuals/companies we have been unable to trace.

These reprints are taken from original copies of each book. in many cases the condition of these originals is not perfect. the publisher has gone to great lengths to ensure the quality of these reprints, but wishes to point out that certain characteristics of the original copies will, of necessity, be apparent in reprints thereof.

British Library Cataloguing in Publication Data
A CIP catalogue record for this book
is available from the British Library

ISBN13: 978-0-415-26921-6 (hbk)

ISBN13: 978-0-415-84618-9 (pbk)

Barriers to Entry and Strategic Competition

Paul Geroski
London Business School

Richard J. Gilbert
University of California, Berkeley, USA

Alexis Jacquemin
Université Catholique de Louvain, Belgium

A volume in the Theory of the Firm and Industrial Organization section

edited by

Alexis Jacquemin
Université Catholique de Louvain, Belgium

harwood academic publishers
chur · london · paris · new york · melbourne

Harwood Academic Publishers

Post Office Box 197
London WC2E 9PX
United Kingdom

58, rue Lhomond
75005 Paris
France

Post Office Box 786
Cooper Station
New York, New York 10276
United States of America

Private Bag 8
Camberwell, Victoria 3124
Australia

Library of Congress Cataloging-in-Publication Data

Geroski, Paul.
Barriers to entry and strategic competition / Paul Geroski, Richard Gilbert, Alexis Jacquemin.
p. cm.—(Fundamentals of pure and applied economics, ISSN 0191-1708; v. 41. Theory of the firm and industrial organization)
Includes bibliographical references.
ISBN 3-7186-5030-4
1. Barriers to entry (Industrial organization) 2. Competition. 3. Industrial concentration. I. Gilbert, Richard, 1945- . II. Jacquemin, Alex. III. Title. IV. Series: Fundamentals of pure and applied economics; v. 41. V. Series: Fundamentals of pure and applied economics. Theory of the firm and industrial organization.
HD2756.5.G47 1990 90-4393
338.6—dc20 CIP

Contents

Introduction to the Series

Drawing on a personal network, an economist can still relatively easily stay well informed in the narrow field in which he works, but to keep up with the development of economics as a whole is a much more formidable challenge. Economists are confronted with difficulties associated with the rapid development of their discipline. There is a risk of "balkanization" in economics, which may not be favorable to its development.

Fundamentals of Pure and Applied Economics has been created to meet this problem. The discipline of economics has been subdivided into sections (listed at the back of this volume). These sections comprise short books, each surveying the state of the art in a given area.

Each book starts with the basic elements and goes as far as the most advanced results. Each should be useful to professors needing material for lectures, to graduate students looking for a global view of a particular subject, to professional economists wishing to keep up with the development of their science, and to researchers seeking convenient information on questions that incidentally appear in their work.

Each book is thus a presentation of the state of the art in a particular field rather than a step-by-step analysis of the development of the literature. Each is a high-level presentation but accessible to anyone with a solid background in economics, whether engaged in business, government, international organizations, teaching, or research in related fields.

Three aspects of *Fundamentals of Pure and Applied Economics* should be emphasized:

—First, the project covers the whole field of economics, not only theoretical or mathematical economics.
—Second, the project is open-ended and the number of books is not predetermined. If new and interesting areas appear, they will generate additional books.

—Last, all the books making up each section will later be grouped to constitute one or several volumes of an Encyclopedia of Economics.

The editors of the sections are outstanding economists who have selected as authors for the series some of the finest specialists in the world.

J. Lesourne *H. Sonnenschein*

Acknowledgements

The authors are obliged to C. Eaton, J. Farrell, D. Fudenberg, R. Masson, J. Panzar, C. Shapiro, P. Regibeau and R. Willig for comments on earlier portions of this work. The usual disclaimer applies. Much of this work relies on Geroski and Jacquemin (1984), Gilbert (1989a), and Geroski (1983).

Barriers to Entry and Strategic Competition

PAUL GEROSKI
London Business School

RICHARD J. GILBERT
University of California, Berkeley, USA

ALEXIS JACQUEMIN
Université Catholique de Louvain, Belgium

I. INTRODUCTION

Entry is a source of competitive discipline on the industrial performance of firms. The threat of entry by new competitors puts a constraint on the latitude of existing firms to conduct their operations in ways that adversely effect consumers, while actual entry changes the structure of markets in ways that often brings about the same ends. Entry, actual or potential, can upset traditional patterns of market conduct, de-throne dominant firms, introduce new technology and fresh approaches to product design and marketing, and lead to more competitive prices.

As agreeable as these consequences of entry may seem to be in principle, there is considerable controversy over the extent to which they are achieved in practice. Observations of actual entry attempts reveal that direct entry typically has only a small effect on industry structure. Masson and Shaanan's [1982] sample of 37 US industries over the period 1950–1966 yielded an average market share penetration by entrants of 4.5% over 6.8 years, a gain of less than 1% per year. Yip [1982], in a sample of 59 entrants in narrowly defined markets, found a median gain of 6% (mean gain = 10%), with entry via acquisition achieving a penetration roughly three times that achieved by direct entrants. Biggadike [1976] investigated 40 entry attempts by 20 large US firms, and observed that less than 40% of these entrants achieved a penetration of at least 10% within two years. Hause and Du Reitz [1984] examined entry in Sweden over a 15 year period and observed that new entrants only managed 1.7% market penetration on average over that period.

Although these figures suggest that entrants manage to make only a fairly modest penetration into most markets, the number of actual entrants that appear in markets is often extremely large. For example, Dunne and Roberts [1986] examined about 400 four-digit US industries in 1967, 1972, 1977 and 1982, and observed 285, 347, 418 and 425 entrants on average per industry respectively. The predominant method of entry was new firms constructing new facilities (e.g. 69% in 1967 and 1982, 74–76% in 1972 and 1977), with diversifying firms numbering between 23–25% (1972, 1977) and 30% (1967 and 1982). In the UK for 1983, Geroski [1988c], observed an average of 197 entrants per three digit industry in 1983–4 (the maximum was 2556), roughly 12% of the stock of existing firms. However, the average gross penetration per entrant per industry was less than 0.1% and the average penetration for all entrants per industry was 5% (the maximum was 26.6%). Further, net import penetration averaged as much as four times the net domestic entry penetration rate.

Even more interesting, it appears from the data that the relationship between entry and exit is surprisingly close. Geroski (1988c) found that, on average, 130 firms exited per industry (the maximum was 1804), leaving a net increase in the number of firms of 67 (the maximum was 1030 and the minimum was − 34), and a net market share penetration of only 2%. There is also evidence to suggest that many of the entrants in year t entered in t − 1, t − 2 and t − 3, and, indeed, that a distressingly high percentage of entrants fail within a year of formation. Net and gross entry penetration and the net and gross number of entrants were each, however, highly positively correlated; the gross number of entrants and gross penetration were mildly negatively correlated. Fairly similar orders of magnitude were observed by Geroski [1988a] for the UK in the 1970s. Baldwin and Gorecki [1983] examined cumulative entry over the period 1970–1979 in 141 Canadian four-digit industries. All entrants post-1970 collectively acquired a market share by 1979 of about 26% on average; entry by birth accounted for 14% and entry by acquisition 12%.

However high this market penetration appears to be, it must be noted that it was accompanied by a large turnover of firms; about 33% of the total 1979 population of firms were not present in 1970, and about 43% of the population of 1970 had, by 1979, disappeared (mainly by scrapping and not divestiture).

Thus, entry appears to be easy but post-entry market penetration and, indeed, survival is not. A question that this raises is whether the somewhat unimpressive market penetration by entrants reflects the existence of generally high barriers to entry in most markets or the differential efficiency advantages of established firms. Barriers to entry are often thought to reflect permanent disadvantages that entrants face, but may also be thought of as a kind of adjustment cost that entrants must overcome. Such adjustment costs can, of course, be affected by the strategic behaviour of incumbents, and this type of consideration broadens the range of potential factors which might account for what we observe. That is, it is of interest to ask whether the low post-entry market penetration that we have observed is caused by high levels of barriers or the strategic behaviour of incumbents, and why so many agents attempt entry when failure rates are high and post entry growth prospects are poor.

Although one may be interested in entry *per se* as an interesting phenomena to explain, the broader concern in looking at entry is, of course, with assessing market performance. If the extent of rivalry amongst active firms in a concentrated industry is too weak to generate a competitive outcome, it is important that new competitors exert a noticeable pressure on prices and productivity in order to have a positive welfare effect. In fact, many scholars believe that the mere anticipation of entry will induce incumbents to lower their prices toward more competitive levels, and thus that entry need not necessarily occur to have an effect on market performance. A benchmark in this respect has been established by Baumol et al [1982] who have applied the label 'perfectly contestable' to markets in which incumbent firms and potential entrants share the same technology and potential competitors can enter and exit without capital loss during the time taken by incumbent firms to change prices.

Formally, Baumol et al [1982] define a 'perfectly contestable market' as a market in which a necessary condition for an equilibrium outcome is that no firm can enter taking prices as given and earn strictly positive profits using the same technology as existing firms. In a perfectly competitive market, entrants can and will enter to take advantage of even transient profit opportunities at current prices. This behaviour is most reasonable when the costs of entry are completely reversible so that there are no capital losses in the event of exit. If these conditions are satisfied, a perfectly contestable market mirrors a competitive environment in which entry and exit are frictionless and barriers to entry and exit are non-existent. The assumption of identical costs insures that whenever incumbents can make profits, so can entrants, and, therefore, if a perfectly competitive market equilibrium exists, firms cannot sustain prices in excess of average cost. If more than one firm operates a positive levels of output in a perfectly contestable market equilibrium, the possibility of incremental changes in the output of a rival firm ensures that, in equilibrium, price cannot deviate from the competitive ideal of marginal cost. Thus, the outcome of competition in a market with unconstrained entry is perfectly competitive whenever the market is not a natural monopoly. If it is a natural monopoly, potential competition ensures that the behaviour of the monopolist is 'regulated' in the sense that total revenues are not more than total costs.

The theory of contestable markets is a useful benchmark to use in analyzing the effect of entry on market performance, but both the theory and its empirical relevance are open to question. A key assumption that is implicit in the theory of perfectly competitive markets is that capital can move with little risk of loss into and out of an industry over a period of time that is short compared to the time required for existing firms to respond with competitive price changes. If this assumption is satisfied, a firm can base its entry decision on current prices, and 'hit and run' can be a rational entry strategy that will police the pricing decisions of incumbent firms. However, it is unlikely that entry into any industry is perfectly reversible; so any entry attempt will probably entail some risk of capital loss if the firm should subsequently exit the industry. Farrell [1986], Gilbert [1986], and Stiglitz [1987] have argued that even if the sunk costs of entry are vanishingly small, the possibility of prompt, aggressive pricing by established firms can make entry unattractive and, by deterring 'hit and run' entry, permit existing firms to price at noncompletitive levels.

Empirical studies of entry also cast doubt on the contestability hypothesis. Many scholars (e.g. Bailey and Baumol [1984]) initially argued that transportation services, and, more specifically, the airline industry, were typical cases of contestable markets where fixed costs, although important, were not sunk because aircraft could be easily diverted to other uses. However, as recognized by Baumol and Willig [1986], several econometric studies have shown that the threat of entry in airline markets does not suffice to keep profits at normal levels (see, e.g., Graham, Kaplan, and Sibley [1983]; Call and Keeler [1985], Morrison and Winston [1987]). The intrinsic mobility of aircraft suggests that entry and exit may be easier in airlines than in most industries, and the fact that pricing in airlines is not determined by the threat of entry provides a good reason to question whether contestability is a force in most industries (see also Schwartz [1986] and Gilbert [1989]). Whether airlines are not contestable because airline fare schedules are capable of being changed with exceptional speed, because ground support facilities are scarce and expenditures on capital other than aircraft are largely sunk costs, or because incumbents are able to deter entry strategically through the use of non-price competitive weapons is not clear. However, the question is important enough to demand both theoretical and empirical work in the different types of entry barrier or deterrence strategies that might be relevant in any particular case.

Contestability theory is an extreme characterization of market performance that relies on the assumption that entry and exit are costless. At the other end of the spectrum is the view that infinitesimal sunk costs are sufficient to protect monopoly behaviour when incumbents respond rapidly and aggressively to entry attempts. In between, there is sufficient ground for divergent views on the effects of potential competition and on the ability of established firms to engage in strategic behaviour that deters entry. The 'structuralist school', typified by the work of Joe Bain [1956], maintains that the efficacy of potential competition depends on determinants of the conditions of entry such as economies of scale, technological advantages, and access to marketing or natural resources. Moreover, members of this school also argue that the conditions of entry can often be manipulated by established firms in various ways to reduce the likelihood that entry will occur and to mitigate its effects. In contrast, the 'Chicago school', typified by the work of Stigler [1968] and Demsetz [1982], maintains that market concentration reflects the differential efficiencies of established firms, and that most of the important types of entry barriers arise from restrictions on market conduct imposed by the government.

Absent these, entry conditions are generally considered to be fairly easy and market performance is generally thought to approximate competitive outcomes fairly closely. Trying to explore the determinants of entry and to ascertain which of these several views about the effect of entry on market performance is most consistent with the facts is not an easy task, and our goal here is to introduce the reader to the basic issues involved in that choice.

We shall proceed through six stages.

Section II presents several different definitions of barriers to entry that have been proposed in the literature. Section III describes Bain's determinants of barriers to entry and introduces the role of behaviour in the determination of the conditions of entry. We adopt Bain's classification of entry barriers as a convenient organizational structure in which to discuss the possible sources of competitive advantage for established firms. This discussion identifies assumptions in Bain's analysis of the conditions of entry that are essential to the predictions of the structuralist school. In particular, the assumed behavioural response of established firms to the entry of rival firms is critical to the likelihood of entry and to the ability of established firms to manipulate the conditions of entry to maintain supra-competitive profits. Our critique in Section III of Bain's classification of the conditions of entry in terms of assumed behavioural responses of incumbent firms attempts to reduce the distinction between the predictions of the structuralist and Chicago schools to different assumptions about firm behaviour. However, the ultimate test of the theory relies on empirical observations and we draw heavily in this section on empirical studies of the conditions of entry and the effects of entry attempts. Section IV calls attention to the importance of exit barriers and specific assets in the theory of capital mobility. Section V describes the theory of dynamic limit pricing, which reflects empirical observations that the conditions of entry can affect the mobility of capital into an industry, but rarely succeed in isolating an industry from entry threats. This is followed in Section VI by a discussion of empirical models that quantify entry conditions, many of which are based on the dynamic limit pricing framework. Section VII contains a few concluding remarks.

II. DEFINITIONS OF MOBILITY BARRIERS

The concept of a 'barrier to entry' is more subtle than it appears to be at first sight. It has proved to be surprisingly difficult to uncover a definition of entry barriers (and more generally, of mobility barriers) that both commands wide acceptance in the profession and is empirically useful. Several alternatives have been proposed, and, in what follows, we summarize some of the more popular candidates. These definitions differ according to their emphasis on the structural characteristics of entry, the consequences of entry for economic performance, and the value of incumbency. While most of the early literature on barriers has focused on impediments to the entry of new capital into a market, we adopt the more general perspective of Caves and Porter [1977] who argue that economic performance depends on limitations to the movement of resources into, out of, or within an existing industry. Thus, we choose to use the more general term of 'mobility barriers.'

A. Structural barriers

The earliest and perhaps most well-known structural definition of barriers to new competition is due to Bain [1956], who argued that the 'condition of entry' is determined '. . . by the advantages of established sellers in an industry over potential entrant sellers' (p. 3), the comparison being made between the pre-entry profits of established firms and post-entry profits of entrants. Thus, a barrier to entry exists if an entrant cannot achieve the profit levels post-entry that the incumbent enjoyed prior to its arrival. Let $\Pi_i(x_1^*, \ldots, x_n^*)$ be incumbent i's profit when incumbent firms $i = 1, \ldots, n$ operate at the pre-entry outputs x_i^*, and let $\Pi_e(x_1^{**}, \ldots, x_n^{**}, x_e^{**})$ be the profit of an entrant at the post-entry outputs x_i^{**} and x_e^{**}. Then, entry is deterred if $\Pi_e < 0$, and Bain's measure of the height of barriers to entry for this industry is $\Pi_i - max\ [\Pi_e, 0]$, the level of profits that can be sustained against entry in perpetuity.

Further, Bain argued that the 'condition of entry is . . . primarily a structural situation . . . [which] describes . . . the circumstances in which the potentiality of competition will or will not become actual' (p. 3; see also pp. 17–18). This additional proviso is intended to rule out transitory phenomena which affect entry from time to time (e.g. trade cycle effects, 'innocently' created entrant misperceptions, and so on), but it does gloss over the possibility that the effects of some structural factors on entry may depend on incumbents' behaviour. In fact, Bain distinguished between the fundamental structural conditions which create symmetries between firms and the strategic behaviour of incumbents which exploit them, but argued that symmetries in outcome ultimately (ie. in the long run) rest on structural factors.

A complicating feature of this definition is that barriers to entry so defined are likely to be specific to the identities of both entrants and incumbents, and what may be a barrier from the point of view of one challenger may not necessarily be so from the point of view of another. For example, it may be the case that the most advantaged challenger is not a new firm, but, rather, one established elsewhere who can use certain assets to overcome what would be barriers for *de novo* firms. Of course, not all those firms or agents who threaten entry actually materialise as entrants in any given period. In order to assess the importance of potential and possibly unobservable entry threats, one needs to decide who the likely challengers are in principle, and how severe are the disadvantages they would suffer from were they to attempt entry. To overcome this type of problem, Bain suggested a counter-factual construction involving the 'most advantaged' potential competitor, leading to a definition of the 'immediate condition of entry' (pp. 9–11) which generates what might best be thought of as an estimate of the minimum height of barriers facing the full population of entrants.[1] To construct this counterfactual entrant, one must know how the best placed agent ought to initiate its entry challenge; that is, one must identify the production, marketing, and distribution strategies that it ought to select. If, after a hypothetical entry by such a firm using such strategies, one finds that it cannot do as well as the incumbent was doing, then, according to Bain, a barrier is said to exist.

B. Stigler and the Chicago School

It is useful to contrast Bain's structural view of barriers to entry with that of Stigler [1968], who proposed that: '. . . a barrier to entry may be

---

[1] Bain went somewhat further than this, defining the 'general condition of entry' as the '. . . succession of values of the immediate condition of entry as entry to the industry occurs . . . beginning with the most favoured firm' (p. 9).

defined as a cost of producing (at some or every rate of output) which must be borne by firms which seek to enter an industry but is not borne by firms already in the industry' (p. 67). Formally, if $C_i(x)$ and $C_e(x)$ are an incumbent's and entrant's cost of producing x, Stigler's measure of the height of a barrier to entry is $C_e(x) - C_i(x)$. The primary conceptual difference between Stigler and Bain is that, in the former case, the entrant and incumbent are compared post-entry: a barrier exists if the two are not equally efficient after the costs of entering the industry are taken into account. Bain's emphasis on the conditions of entry assign an entry barrier to any industry in which structural conditions exist that permit an established firm to elevate price above the minimum average cost of potential entrants. Stigler considers an entry barrier to exist only if the conditions of entry were less difficult for established firms than for new entrants.

There are some difficulties with Stigler's definition. His reference to 'some or every rate of output' makes the definition ambiguous. Should the barrier to entry be measured at the point of minimum efficient scale, at the incumbent's present output, or the entrant's expected output? These quantities are likely to differ, and, therefore, Stigler's measure of the size of the entry barrier can be arbitrary.[2] Exactly what Stigler means by 'costs that must be borne' is not clear. Does this include costs incurred by incumbent firms that have become sunk costs? Stigler's measure is also, as in Bain, specific to the identity of both entrant and incumbent. His focus on costs appears to ignore revenue-dependent sources of entry barriers, such as product differentiation, but, in fact, Stigler's definition is generalisable in a straightforward way to include whatever costs an entrant might have to bear to overcome a product differentiation advantage of an incumbent firm. According to Stigler's (somewhat generalized) definition, a barrier to entry would exist if the new firm has to overcome more consumer resistance than did the established firm. The height of an entry barrier would be the additional cost an entrant would have to bear in order to produce the same revenue as an established firm.

---

[2] Stigler's reference to some *or every* rate of output raises questions that seem outside the scope of entry of barriers. Suppose that an entrant has costs that are identical to an incumbent except for outputs that would not be produced. If entry is otherwise easy, this should not contribute to entry barriers. Note that if Stigler had restricted his definition to costs measured at the incumbent's pre-entry output, the definition would address the question of whether an entrant could replicate an incumbent's production at equal costs. This is a necessary (but not sufficient) condition for a perfectly contestable market.

The practical distinction between Bain and Stigler lies in the evaluation of economies of scale as a barrier to entry. Economies of scale are a barrier to entry according to Bain because if scale economies are important, then entry is likely to lead to a price reduction, and, even if entry were successful, profits to the entrant post-entry are likely to be lower as a consequence than they were to the incumbent pre-entry. However, under Stigler's definition, scale economies do not represent a barrier to entry if they imply penalties from suboptimal levels of production that are the same for both established firms and potential entrants. According to Stigler, if an entrant incurs a higher cost because it must produce at a lower level of output, the cost disadvantage is a consequence of demand conditions in the market and not the existence of a barrier to entry. '. . . some economists will say that economies of scale are a barrier to entry meaning that economies explain why no additional firms enter. It would be equally possible to say that inadequate demand is a barrier to entry' (Stigler, 1968, p. 67).

C. A normative definition of barriers

Both Bain and Stigler's approach to the definition of a barrier to entry is positive. Their definitions do not address the welfare consequences of entry, but, instead, characterize conditions that impede entry. Von Weizsacker has attempted to approach the definition of barriers to entry from a normative point of view. His concern is not with the factors that impede the mobility of capital, but rather with 'socially undersirable limitations to entry of resources which are due to protection of resource owners already in the market' (von Weizsacker [1980], p. 13). Von Weizsacker's definition of barriers to entry is a qualification of the definition proposed by Stigler. Von Weizsacker defines a barrier to entry as 'a cost of producing (at some or every rate of output) which must be borne by firms which seek to enter an industry but is not borne by firms already in the industry, and which implies a distortion in the use of economic resources form the social point of view.' (. 400) The definition implies that there could be too little entry due to excessive protection, and also that there could be too much entry due to too little protection.

Consider the following simple example. Suppose a large number of firms have a cost function $C(x) = mx + F$, where F is sunk if entry occurs. The inverse demand function is $P(X) = a - bX$, where X is total demand and is equal in equilibrium to the total supply by all firms. The first best allocation in this market calls for one firm producing at an output at which $P = m$. However entry will occur until the profit of the $(n+1)$st firm is negative. Suppose all firms that are active in the industry behave as Cournot competitors. Each firm produces $(a-m)/(b(n+1))$, total output is $n(a-m)/(b(n+1))$, and there are too many firms relative to the first best allocation. Of course, adding more firms to the market increases total output, but, relative to the total output with $n-1$ firms, total output increases by only $(a-m)/(bn(n+1))$, which is only $1/n$ of the sales of the nth firm. It is not difficult to show that if one could control only the number of firms in the market, the number that maximizes total economic surplus would be less than the number of firms in a market equilibrium. New entrants ignore the negative externality that they impose on existing firms, and, thus, there is too much entry.[3] Conditions that increase the cost of entry into this market could increase economic surplus and would not be barriers to entry from von Weizsacker's normative perspective.

If an activity creates positive externalities, the entrepreneur organizing it can be insufficiently protected by property rights so that there would be insufficient incentive to devote resources to this activity. For example, if patents do not provide enough protection for investors, too few resources would be devoted to investment in R & D. On the other hand, if an activity causes negative externalities, it can be excessively protected. Excessive patent protection, for example, could result in excessive inventive activity for the same reason. According to von Weiszacker, a barrier exists only if the equilibrium involves insufficient entry relative to the social optimum. Demsetz [1982] has further extended this normative approach to the evaluation of barriers to entry by arguing that, in many cases, what is called an entry barrier is an endogenous response to consumer preferences and supports an efficient allocation of resources. For example, the number of brands may be limited by consumers' ability to evaluate different alternatives. Entry is restained by consumers' reluctance to assume additional

---

[3] These results follows the excess capacity argument in Chamberlin [1933]. For a more detailed discussion, see Dixit and Stiglitz [1977], Perry [1984], Mankiw and Whinston [1986], or Gilbert and Vives [1986].

information cost. Rather than allowing resources into high profit industries, it might be better to take into account the role of externalities, information and transaction costs, and to consider entry barriers as a valuable second best answer to real world frictions: '... existing firms have an advantage insofar as their existence commands loyalty ... (that is barriers) reflect lower real cost of transacting, industry specific investments, or reputable history (which is) an asset to the firm possessing it because information is not free ...' (pp. 50–1).[4]

The major strength of this approach—it's explicit focus on the normative consequences of entry—is also the source of its major weakness. It is difficult enough to measure barriers to entry (defined à la Bain or Stigler) without adding an additional layer of normative complexity, and it is probably simpler to evaluate barriers in two explicit steps: first, measure their height, and then, second, evaluate their consequences for welfare.

D. The value of incumbency

In contrast to the normative approach to the determination of mobility barriers, Gilbert [1989a] concentrates solely on the advantages that accrue to established firms. According to Gilbert, a mobility barrier exists if firm earns rents (which may be negative) as a consequence of incumbency. Let Π_i^k be the profit of the ith incumbent firm in industry k and let Π_i^l be the profit that firm i could earn if it were to abandon industry k and enter an alternative industry 1. Included in the set of alternative industries is the null industry of doing nothing, and this set could include k, in which case the incumbent would be a new entrant in its own industry. In the latter case, the hypothetical exit and re-entry should occur after remaining incumbent firms have had time to adjust to the exit of the firm. An incumbency rent exists if $\Pi_i^k > max(1)\ \Pi_i^l$, and the magnitude of this difference is a measure of the incumbency rent. This definition has no relation to the consequences of entry or exit for economic welfare. The emphasis is on the role of history and how that affects relative profits; an entry barrier exists if a firm earns a

[4] Compare this with Stiglitz [1981] who argues that in precisely this case where markets are incomplete, information is costly, and, where R & D expenditures are important, increases in competition may have adverse effects on welfare.

premium by virtue of its being established in the industry. An exit barrier exists if an incumbent firm could earn more if it could leave the industry.

This definition is similar to that used by Bain, but is has some important differences. It does not depend on the identity of an entrant firm, because only the incumbent firm's technology is considered. There are, however, as many values of incumbency as there are incumbent firms, and these values may span a wide range. It also deals with the question of opportunity costs of scarce factors. If the incumbent were to abandon the industry, one option it has is to sell its factors of production or to use them in a different activity, and this consideration means that they must be valued at their opportunity costs. A potential criticism of this definition of incumbency rents is that obvious sources of competitive advantage are likely to be discounted because they have values that capitalize monopoly profits. For example, a key patent need not be a source of incumbency rents if it can be sold for a price that equals its value to the current owner. But, as Section III.B discusses more fully, there are reasons not to call a patent an entry barrier if it has an opportunity cost equal to its value to the patentee, any more than a scarce piece of land should be considered a barrier to entry.

Most of the literature on capital mobility limits attention to the flow of physical capital into and out of an industry. Entry is 'easy' if an entrepreneur can move factors of production into an industry and earn profits that are comparable to the profits earned by incumbent firms. However this ignores the possibility of entry through acquisition of existing assets. Most of the entry literature has tended to ignore this avenue of entry, perhaps because entry by acquisition does not add to the productive resources of the industry. However, the opportunity to acquire an existing firm is an alternative to direct entry and this action can have real consequences for economic performance (see Gilbert and Newbery [1988]). The definition of barriers to entry as a rent to incumbency can incorporate entry by acquisition if one of the alternative activities available to an incumbent firm is the direct sale of its corporate assets. One should, however, note that the price of entry by acquisition need not be less than the price of direct entry by new capital investment in an industry. Entry by acquisition can be impeded by the managers of incumbent firms, who may place an asking price on corporate assets that exceed their value to new management. A reason why managers may refuse to sell out even if 'the price is right' is that managers have firm-specific capital that is invested in their firm. But, as Gilbert and Newbery [1988] argue, potential entrants may be able to acquire incumbent firms at favourable terms by threatening to enter as rivals if the target firms refuse to sell.

This review of the different approaches that have been taken to the identification and measurement of mobility barriers reveals that there is considerable controversy over what is a barrier to entry and how it should be measured. Economies of scale can be a significant barrier to entry according to Bain, insignificant according to Stigler, and von Weizsacker might argue that economies of scale do not prevent enough entry from occurring! In what follows, we will attempt to resolve some of the differences between the conclusions of Bain and Stigler, showing how the consequences for capital mobility of factors such as economies of scale depend critically on the behaviour of incumbent firms. This is consistent with our view of barriers to capital mobility as determining rents that are derived form incumbency. The size of these rents will depend on the behaviour of established firms. We will not attempt to perform a welfare analysis of barriers to capital mobility, but will remain content to alert the reader to the distinction between the positive and normative consequences of factors that might impede the flow of capital into and out of markets.

III. DETERMINANTS OF THE CONDITION OF ENTRY

Bain [1956] identified economies of scale, product differentiation, and absolute cost advantages of established firms as the major determinants of the conditions of entry. This taxonomy provides a convenient jumping-off point for a discussion of sources of barriers to capital mobility, and we shall consider each type of barrier in turn. However, it will be evident that the extent to which these factors actually impede capital mobility depends on industry behaviour, and, therefore, that they cannot be evaluated without taking into account the strategic actions that are available to established firms. The interactions between Bain's sources of barriers to capital mobility and firm behaviour also imply that established firms may be able to enhance the deterrence value of structural barriers to capital mobility by engaging in strategic behaviour designed to make entry more difficult. Some of the ways in which this can be accomplished, and some of the obstacles to strategic exploitation of mobility barriers, are discussed below.

A. Barriers and strategic behaviour

Potential competitors will be reluctant to enter an industry if they anticipate that incumbents will respond to entry by competing aggressively for market share. Sophisticated incumbents who anticipate potential competition may attempt to signal an aggressive stance, perhaps by cutting prices before entry occurs (e.g., see the classic paper by Modigliani, [1958]). This type of strategy—often called 'limit pricing'—captures the very reasonable notion that the presence of potential competitors can have an effect on price determination, and that strategic actions undertaken by incumbents may pre-empt and thus deter entrants. However, while intuitively appealing, the problem with this type of argument is that it is a little too simple. In the presence of complete information, there is no reason why the price that prevails before entry should have, by itself, an influence on the decisions of a potential entrant. The success of such a strategy depends on the extent to which potential rivals correlate pre-entry behaviour to post-entry profits. Streeten [1955], for example, argued that 'the absence of excess profits will have an entirely different effect upon rivals contemplating entry according to whether it indicates an absence of profit opportunities, or a reluctance to exploit them. The latter will only have the effect of the former if it succeeds as a bluff . . . If we assume that potential entrants see through the bluff, the absence of excess profits will be no deterrent to entry' (p. 261). Put otherwise, the pre-entry strategic action is unlikely to create an advantage for the incumbent in a situation where one does not already exist. Rather, it is designed to exploit structural asymmetries between entrant and incumbent, particularly in situations where the size of these are not well understood by the entrant.

The use of price as a signal of post-entry market conditions in conditions of incomplete information has been discussed more recently by Salop [1979] and posed in game-theoretic form by Milgrom and Roberts [1982a]. In the Milgrom and Roberts model, uncertainty is limited to entrants' knowledge of an incumbent's marginal production cost. Entry is assumed to be profitable if the incumbent has a high cost, but unprofitable if its cost is low, and they assume that the expected value of entry is negative, so entry would occur only if the potential entrant anticipates that the incumbent has a high cost. They show that there may exist a 'separating equilibrium', in which the incumbent's pre-entry price is a function of its marginal production cost. Only in such an equilibrium does price serve as a signal of post-entry profitability. Although entry occurs if an incumbent is high cost in a separating equilibrium, the incumbent's price is lower as a consequence of entrants' imperfect information. Hence they conclude that the incumbent engages in limit pricing, but that it does not prevent entry when entry would be profitable. In effect, the purpose of limit pricing in the Milgrom and Roberts model is to prevent potential rivals from thinking that the incumbent firm has even higher costs than it actually has.

The consequences of imperfect information for entry deterrence depend on the information structure of the game between entrants and incumbents. Matthews and Mirman [1983], Saloner [1981], and Harrington [1984] describe signalling models in which prices are noisy signals of market conditions. As a result of exogenous disturbances, a potential entrant is not able to determine post-entry market conditions with certainty given an incumbent's pricing decision. These models show that, in a noisy information model, the probability of entry can be an increasing function of an incumbent's price (which provides a theoretical foundation for models of limit pricing such as Kamien and Schwartz [1971] and Gaskins [1971] discussed below in Section V). Moreover, the probability of entry depends on the information structure of the model, and may differ from the probability of entry that would occur with perfect information about market conditions. An extension of the Milgrom and Roberts model by Harrington [1984] illustrates the importance of these points. Harrington allows the entrant's cost function to be uncertain and positively correlated with the incumbent's cost (not unreasonable if they use similar production technologies). If the potential entrant believes its costs is high, it will stay out of the industry. With the different twist of positively correlated costs, the incumbent has an incentive to price high in order to signal a high cost and thereby convince the entrant that its cost is high too. In order to discourage entry, the incumbent prices high, not low!

Related to the theory of price as a signal of the conditions of entry are dynamic models of repeated games in which established firms can influence entrants' expectations of post-entry competitive conditions through their choice of pre-entry pricing strategies. These games include Selten's [1978] discussion of pricing by a chain store and the reputation models developed by Kreps and Wilson [1982] and Milgrom [1982]. These models rely on some degree of asymmetric information about incumbents' behaviour in the post-entry market. A potential entrant may be unsure as to whether established firms will accommodate new entry or price aggressively in response to an entry attempt. These models show that even a small prior expectation by the entrant that an incumbent will respond to entry in an aggressive manner may be sufficient to encourage an incumbent to take an aggressive stance and reinforce the entrant's expectations.

Strategic behaviour of incumbents is essential to the consequences for entry of most structural characteristics of markets. For example, suppose all firms have the cost function $C(x) = mx + F$. If industry behaviour is such that two or more firms act as perfect competitors, then entry would result in price equal to marginal cost and no firm would earn a profit. The only sustainable market structure would be a monopoly. Contrast this with a situation where incumbent firms always chose to keep their prices unchanged in response to entry. In the latter case, if price exceeds average cost, entry may be feasible even in an industry that is a natural monopoly. Thus, a theory of barriers to entry cannot be constructed in isolation from a theory of oligopoly behaviour.

B. Scale economies, sunk costs and limit pricing

According to Bain, economies of scale create problems for entrants in two ways, via a 'percentage effect' and an 'absolute capital requirements effect' (Bain, [1956], p. 55). The former depends on the size of the minimum efficient scale plant relative to the extent of the market, and occurs for large minimum efficient plants (MEP hereafter) because, if the entrant is to enter at efficient scale, the '. . . addition to going industry output . . . will result in a reduction of industry selling prices' (p. 53) for any reasonable response by incumbents. If entry occurs at less than efficient scale, the entrant will face a cost penalty depending on the slope of the cost curve at sub-MEP scales. Note that implicit in Bain's conclusion about the percentage effect of large MEP plants is the prescription that incumbents firms will not accommodate entry by scaling back their own production by an amount equal to the production offered by new entrants. Under the hypothesis of perfectly contestable markets, a potential entrant conjectures that market prices would be unaffected by its entry, which corresponds to a situation in which established firms do accommodate new entrants. In contrast, a competitive response to entry implies an increase in post-entry output. The key question is, therefore, the extent to which potential entrants expect that incumbent firms will act to hold onto market share.

Bain's 'absolute capital requirements effect' arises from the large investment outlays necessary to build an appropriate sized plant (given capital market imperfections), and the size of the disadvantage so created is liable to depend on the absolute size of MEP. Implicit in this source of barrier to capital mobility is a view that new entrants will encounter difficulties in raising capital, locating and training a qualified workforce, and developing the inventories and distribution channels needed for entry at MES. These differential cost effects are discussed in more detail in the next section.

Estimating scale-related entry barriers involves generating estimates of the cost per unit that could be achieved at different output scales by the most advantaged entrant (i.e. one using the best possible organization of production currently available and minimizing factor expenditures). The major problem is that 'the best possible' is often difficult to observe. What can be easily observed are the actual unit costs of incumbent firms or the actual distribution of plant sizes, and a great temptation exists to infer 'ought' (i.e. the cost of the best-practice plant) from 'is' (i.e. those actually prevailing)[5]. What is needed to make this alternative approach work is the ability to isolate and identify those existing plants which most nearly approximate the best production process that can be implemented under the circumstances. The four following techniques all follow this procedure, making the implicit assumption that one or all existing firms are efficient, and that the best an entrant can do is to replicate their actions.

[5] These efforts are generally justified by noting the high correlations which exist between the different proxies of MEP (e.g. Scherer, [1980] p. 95, footnote 45). Since such correlations can hide important differences in size, and fail to reveal measurement errors systematically associated with a number of features of market structure, this happy congruence of measurements ought not to be pushed too far.

The simplest and most direct principle of plant selection originated with Bain (1956, p. 69), who postulated that: '. . . the largest plants are likely to be at least as large as is required for maximum efficiency . . .', because the firms operating the largest plants are typically multiplant firms, and these firms have the option of building a plant to optimal size before they elect to build another plant at a different location. Of course, such a criteria does not give an estimate of MEP if the true average cost curve has a substantial flat segment. What is more, it is not obvious how large a firm must be in order to be free from constraints in the choice of plant size, nor whether such firms are sufficiently disciplined by market forces to seek the true minimum cost position; further, mistakes can lead to plant sizes that are too large. Consequently, it should not come as too much of a surprise to find that this approach generates a fairly wide range of predictions of MEP depending on different notions of 'how large is large, but still efficient'. Bain computed the average size of all plants in the largest Census of Production size class, and numerous others have been introduced subsequently and used over the years: the average industry plant size as a proxy for MEP, the mid-point of the size distribution (i.e. that plant size above which is produced 50% of industry output), and the average size of the largest plants responsible for 50% of industry output.[6] Lyons [1980] suggested an alternative proxy which is an interesting contrast to these five. Using a rather stronger argument about plant selection than Bain, he concluded that firms producing at the true MEP will be equally likely to operate one or two plants, and thus that MEP can be identified by looking at the actual plant sizes of those firms who, on average, operate about 1.5 plants.

As an alternative to the direct measurement of plant cost functions, one can use a 'selection of the fittest' principle to identify the efficient

[6] Quite often such measures are used to 'explain' concentration levels. Since plant and firm size distributions are almost tautologically related (the complication is multiplant operation), and since error in measurement involved in using such proxies for MEP are liable to be highly correlated to concentration levels, this seems a dubious practice at best (e.g. Davies, [1980]). Caves *et al.* [1975] propose a modification of such measures, trying to pinpoint those industries with both steep costs curves and large minimum efficient plants. Essentially, this involves multiplying or otherwise modifying estimates of MEP with a dummy variable which takes the value of unity when the ratio of the value added per worker in small plants to that in large plants is 'small', since: . . . 'under certain assumptions the reported variations in value added per worker with scale of establishment will provide an inverse measure of variations in average unit cost . . .'. (pp. 133)

size class from the existing size distribution of firms. This approach identifies efficiency with the ability to survive and prosper: '. . . an efficient size of firm is one that meets any and all problems the entrepreneur actually faces . . .' (Stigler, [1958], p. 73). There are obviously several empirical criteria one could use to pick out such 'winners'. They are likely to be relatively profitable (and probably persistently so), and so one could choose MEP as that size of firm whose market share yielded the highest profit (this could be read off regressions such as those of Shepherd [1972], although Shepherd does not use this interpretation; however, see Scherer, [1980], p. 92). Alternatively, efficient firms could be those with high growth, investment, share prices and so on. However, it is generally agreed that the most plausible approach is to trace developments over time in market shares associated with different sized firms, (for obvious reasons, it is difficult to apply this technique to plants), and what have come to be labelled as 'survivor technique estimates' are generated by the following rule proposed by Stigler [1958]: '. . . if the share of a given (size) class falls, it is relatively inefficient, and in general is more inefficient the more rapidly share falls' (p. 73), (pp. 75–6). Thus, the procedure defines L-shaped cost curves whose 'kink' (MEP) is determined by that size class whose market share does not decline. In principle, such estimates have little to say about efficiency as it is conventionally used (they refer to: '. . . the decisive meaning of efficiency from the viewpoint of the enterprise. Of course, social efficiency may be a very different thing', p. 73), they are liable to be accurate indications of entry problems only for entrants who could exactly replicate the competitive conditions of incumbents in the size class they choose to enter, and they are liable to confound market power and cost effectiveness. In practice (e.g. Saving [1961], Weiss [1964], Rees [1973]: for a critique, see Shepherd [1967]), such estimates of MEP are not always stable over time, are not always unique, are very sensitive to market definitions, and problems can arise because the notion of 'survivability' is not easy to define precisely (is a 2% market share decline random noise, measurement error, or indicative of a real loss of competitive edge?).

Progress from the quality of the proxies generated thus far can only come from better, more extensive data used with perhaps more precise conceptualizations of how efficiency varies with scale. Two possibilities in this direction are 'statistical cost estimates' and 'production or cost function estimates'. The former construct estimates of industry cost functions from observations on the unit costs of plants producing different output rates (e.g. Johnston [1960] and many others). Aside from a myriad of difficulties to be faced in accurately measuring costs, there is a major conceptual problem involved in assuming that all incumbents operate on the common average cost curve so estimated (i.e. the principle of plant selection implicitly involved is that *all* industry incumbents are efficient). While this may not bias estimates of MEP, it is certain to give a fairly murky picture of the cost disadvantages of producing at sub or super optimal scale. Thus, for example, high cost observations of small plants may reflect a steeply sloped common industry cost curve, *or* may reflect the inefficiency of those firms not cost competitive enough to gain a healthy market share. To take a second example, in a homogeneous goods industry where all firms operate as Cournot competitors with the same constant average cost function, one will observe one point on the cost curve, and this creates the erroneous impression of a single unique production capacity plant. The general point (which, of course, applies to all of the proxies discussed thus far) is that the use of observed costs (or plant sizes) to infer best practice costs cannot proceed without a critical awareness of how the data were generated. Much the same problem plagues production or cost function estimates which use basic data on factor inputs and expenditures to generate estimates of MEP given *a priori* assumptions on the industry wide commonality of production techniques, and its characteristics.[7]

All of the techniques discussed above share the common weakness identified at the outset; viz that in order to apply these numbers to describe the entry problems facing the most advantaged entrant, one has to imagine that certain (or all) incumbents are efficient, and that entrants can do no better than to replicate the decisions of these firms. This is an important shortcoming, and it is necessary to consider the far more expensive alternative of direct measurement of MEP. Here one has little choice except to simply work out from basic engineering principles what would be the optimal plant size (given current technology, factor prices, and so on) for an entrant to aspire to, and how large

[7] Production and their dual cost function estimates gain the ability to pinpoint production function parameters by relying heavily on the assumption of profit maximization. The cost is that estimates of such parameters are sensitive to th measurement of marginal revenue which, in turn, means that they are sensitive tc assumptions made about oligopolistic interactions; e.g. see the results of Gollop and Roberts, 1979.

the various cost penalties associated with non-optimal scale are. Provided that such information is actually available at a not too unreasonable cost to potential entrants, one could imagine an entrant doing exactly this and, for this reason, one might argue that such 'engineering' estimates '. . . undoubtedly provide the best single source of information on the cost-scale question' (Scherer, [1980], p. 94; for applications and extensive discussions of the technique, see Bain, [1956], Scherer *et al.*, [1975], and Pratten, [1971]). From the work which has thus far been done (on samples biased towards industries believed to have large MEPs), it seems that MEP is fairly modest relative to market size, at least in economies like the U.S. with large low transport cost markets, or those with well developed export links (Scherer, [1980], pp. 96–7). Given at least a moderate target market share by entrants, entry difficulties due to scale economies in production or distribution may well be more the exception than the rule.[8]

Scale advantages can also arise on the demand side, from advantages which large firms enjoy in generating revenue. An interesting possibility in this respect arises in connection with advertising, and the debate on this particular subject is extensive (e.g. see Comanor and Wilson [1979]). Economies of scale may arise from thresholds in the effect of advertising on sales, from variations in rate structures with respect to size of advertising budget, and from variations in the effectiveness of different media (e.g. television vs the rest) whose use requires expenditures of different orders of magnitude. Evidence from both beer [Peles, 1971] and cigarettes [Brown, 1978] lend support to the notion that such economies exist. Brown, for example, calculated that a new entrant would be required to achieve an advertising-sales ratio nearly 50% higher than that of incumbent firms to enable it to compete on a par.

Estimates of MEP that are large or small in any particular market do not necessarily imply that barriers to mobility are large or small in that

[8] The generally very poor industrial relations record of large plants (e.g. Masters, [1969], Scherer, [1976], Prais, [1978]) is at least one additional reason to be suspicious of the efficiency claims for scale implicit in high estimates of MEP, since engineering estimates generally take no real account of such factors. Engineering estimates have also been used to make inferences about multi-plant economies and minimum efficient size of firm (MEF). Scherer *et al.* [1975], in a comprehensive study of 12 industries, found scant evidence from engineering estimates to suggest that multiplant operations generate much more than a 'slight' cost advantage.

market, partly because the cost disadvantage of operating at sub-MEP scale may be only slight, and partly because the effects of entry on price at efficient scale depend on incumbents' behaviour. Bain [1956], Sylos-Labini [1962], Modigliani [1958], and others have investigated the ability of incumbent firms to exploit the scale advantages of the 'percentage effect' originating from MEP, and their work has led to the classic 'limit-pricing' model of behaviour by a dominant firm or cartel. The model, which was originally proposed by Bain and Sylos-Labini and formalized by Modigliani (henceforth referred to as the BSM model), assumes that a dominant firm or cartel establishes an output which potential entrants expect will continue to be produced if entry occurs. This assumption, which the authors proposed as a conservative conjecture on the part of potential competitors, implies that new entrants face a residual inverse demand $P(X_o + X_e)$, where X_o is the unchanged output of the dominant firm and X_e is the entrant's output. In effect, the entrant's inverse demand function is 'shifted to the right' by the amount X_o, and this gives incumbents the opportunities to affect the entrant's expected post-entry profits. A firm cannot profit from entry if, given the incumbent output and the expectations of the potential entrant, the market price is below the entrant's average

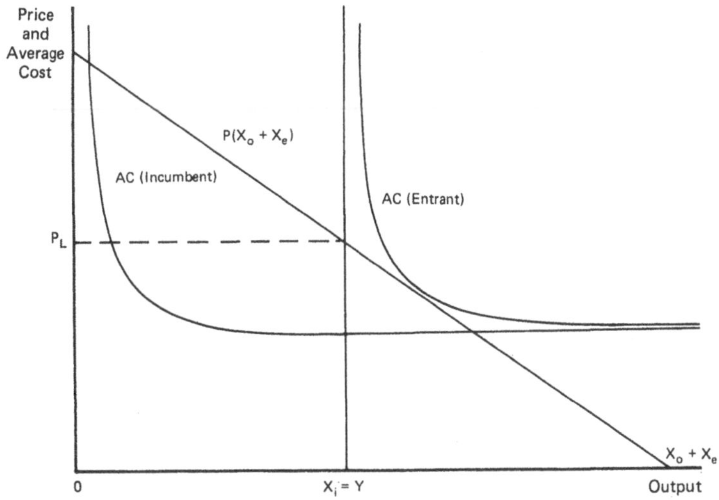

FIGURE 1 Limit pricing.

cost at any feasible level of output. This condition is illustrated in Figure 1.

The BSM model assumes that potential entrants are pessimistic in their entry expectations. They act on the belief that incumbent firms will be able to maintain their pre-entry sales if entry occurs. Bain labels a situation where the optimal output of incumbent firm(s), without regard to the threat of entry, is sufficient to make entry unprofitable, as one of 'blockaded' entry. A situation where incumbent firm(s) earn higher profits by choosing an output at which entry is prevented than they would earn if entry is allowed, is called 'effectively impeded' entry. The converse is 'ineffectively impeded entry'.

The 'limit price' and 'limit output' are determined by demand and the entrant's technology. Figure 2 shows the incumbents' optimal output as a function of the limit output, Y.[9] Region B in Figure 2 corresponds to blockaded entry, which occurs if the incumbents' optimal output ignoring entry, X_o, exceeds the limit output, Y. The smallest limit output for which incumbents maximize profits by allowing entry strictly exceeds X_o. This follows because if entry occurs, the new firm produces a strictly positive output, which means that incumbent firms suffer a non-negligible loss of market share. Thus, incumbent firms are willing to incur losses relative to the unconstrained output in order to deter entry. If the limit output were equal to X_o, the optimal output ignoring entry, the cost to incumbents of increasing output to deter entry would be nil. By continuity, the limit output at which entry is allowed must strictly exceed X_o. Moreover, at the limit output for which the incumbent is indifferent between preventing and allowing entry, total output is strictly lower and price is strictly higher when entry is allowed.

This condition must hold because, if incumbent firms allowed entry to occur, they would lose market share. In order to be indifferent between having all of the market (with no entry) and part of the market (with entry), the price must be higher in the latter case. Thus, when established firms act to limit entry of new competitors, price should be lower, and economic welfare may be higher, than if established firms accommodated new entrants.

---

[9] The limit output is treated as a parameter in Figure 2, but it need not be outside the influence of the incumbent firms(s). Williamson [1963] describes the use of marketing expenditures to influence limit prices. Expenditures that effect factor prices (see Williamson [1968] and Salop and Scheffman [1983]) may affect limit prices as well.

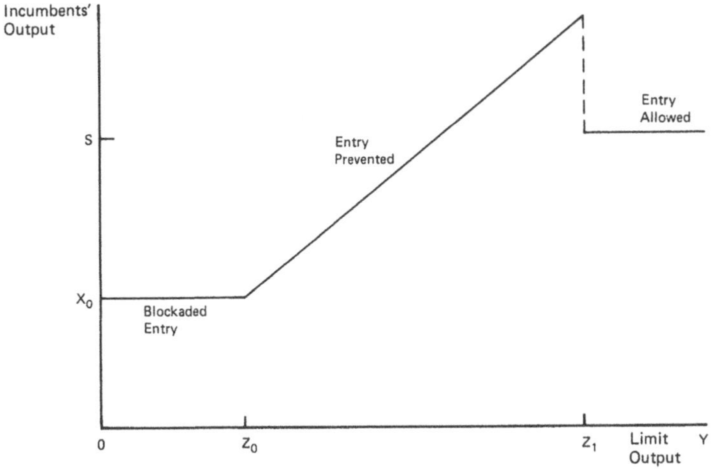

FIGURE 2 Zones of strategic behavior.

The assumption that incumbent firms can convince potential entrants that they will continue to produce at the pre-entry output level regardless of whether or not entry occurs was recognized as crucial early in the development of the theory of limit pricing. One can easily see that alternative assumptions profoundly affect the scope for limit pricing. For example, suppose that the potential entrant conjectures that if it were to enter the market, it would compete with established firms as a Cournot oligopolist. In making its decision to enter, the entrant cares only about profits in the post-entry game. It will chose to enter if the incumbents' Cournot equilibrium output is less than the limit output, and will stay out of the market otherwise. If the established firm's pre-entry price and output have no bearing on the equilibrium of the post-entry game, they will properly be disregarded by the potential entrant. The incumbent might as well set the monopoly price in the pre-entry period, for any other choice would sacrifice profits in the pre-entry period with no consequences for the likelihood of entry. Limit pricing will not occur. Of course, Cournot competition is not the only plausible scenario for the post-entry game. Spence [1977] examined a limit-pricing model in which he assumed that the post-entry game was perfectly competitive, which implies that the post-entry price equals (the lowest) marginal cost of the competitors. Again, pre-entry output is no longer an indication of post-entry profitability and the limit pricing model breaks down. Spence argued that incumbent firms may invest in additional production capacity in order to lower their post-entry marginal cost and therefore lower the post-entry price and profitability for the entrant. Because the pre-entry price is not a signal of post-entry profitability, the incumbents can choose the monopoly price in the pre-entry stage, given their production costs. These alternatives to the BSM model differ in their assumptions about the *behaviour* of the firms in the industry, and, in particular, about the *beliefs* that firms have about how their rivals will behave. As these beliefs should be based on realistic expectations of the consequences of entry decisions, it is interesting to ask how established firms can convince potential entrants that actions such as limit pricing which are intended to discourage entry will indeed make entry unprofitable if it is attempted. We explore two different ways in which established firms can send *credible* signals to potential rivals that discourage entry. The first derives from the characteristics of the entrant's production technology, while the second depends on asymmetric information about production costs.

The output commitment in the BSM model is credible if established firms would choose to maintain their pre-entry total output if entry should occur. The ability to credibly commit is related to the concept of 'subgame perfection' in the theory of dynamic games. A strategy, which defines the reaction of firms to the actions of their competitors and the random occurrences of nature (see Selten [1975] and Kreps and Wilson [1982]). Included in this possible spectrum of games is the game corresponding to the entry of a new competitor. Thus, a strategy in which established firms act to maintain their collective output in the face of entry is a subgame perfect equilibrium strategy (and hence credible) if it is an equilibrium choice of the established firms whether or not entry occurs.[10]

When capital expenditures, once made, become irreversible or 'sunk' in the next period, an established firm might be able to commit to producing an output that it could not sustain as an equilibrium if its

[10] Note that it is the strategy, and not an output, which is subjected to the test of subgame perfection. The strategy defines how established firms would respond to the action of their competitors. The strategy is credible if it results in a constant output if entry occurs.

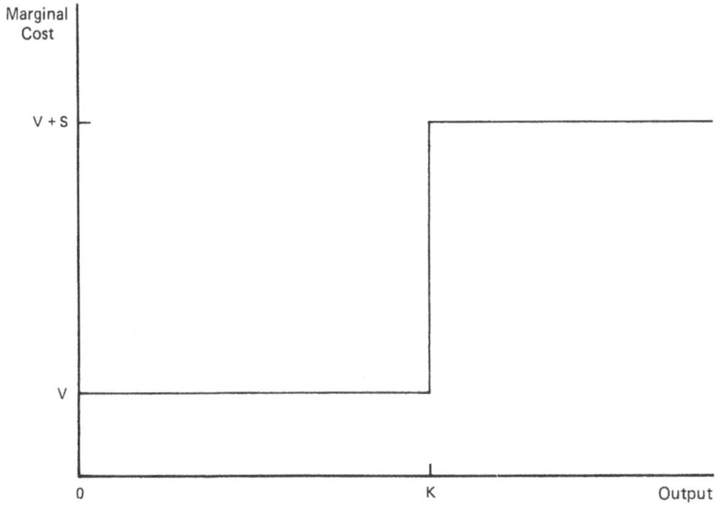

FIGURE 3 Marginal cost function with sunk costs.

first period expenditure were reversible. The existence of sunk expenditures has the effect of lowering the incumbent's marginal cost for any output below the full capacity level of output, which, in turn, discourages the firm from cutting output in response to entry. This argument is due to Dixit [1981], who proposed the following simple model. Dixit allows production cost to depend on installed capacity, K, in addition to output. Both are measured in the same units (e.g. tons/yr of output and tons/yr of capacity). Capacity has a cost of s per unit and, once installed, has no alternative use. The cost function is

$$\begin{aligned} C(x, K) &= vx + sK + F \qquad \text{for } x < K, \\ &= (v + s)x + F \qquad \text{for } x = K. \end{aligned} \tag{1}$$

The marginal cost function (1) is shown in Figure 3. Marginal cost is v whenever there is excess to capacity, and $v + s$ when capacity and output are equal. F remains as a reversible fixed cost.

The incumbent has sunk costs of sK, but a potential entrant has no sunk costs because it has not yet invested in capacity. As the entrant will built just enough capacity to produce its anticipated output, the entrant's cost function is simply

$$C(x) = (v + s)x + F. \tag{2}$$

The Cournot–Nash reaction functions corresponding to the cost functions in (1) for the incumbent and (2) for the potential entrant are shown in Figure 4. The reaction function labelled $R^i(x_e/m)$ is the incumbent's reaction function when the firm has no excess capacity (that is, when $K = x_i$), so that its marginal cost is $v + s = m$. If $K > x_i$, the incumbent's marginal cost is only v and its reaction curve is $R^i(x_e/v)$, which is to the right of the reaction function with no excess capacity. The reaction function that the incumbent is 'on' depends upon the installed capacity and its output x_i. The entrant has no installed capacity. Therefore, with respect to its entry decision, the entrant faces a marginal cost of $v + s$, which includes the cost of capacity. The entrant's reaction function is shown as $R^e(x_i/m)$ in Figure 4.

If the incumbent has no installed capacity, its reaction function is $R^i(x_e/m)$ and the Cournot equilibrium occurs at the point $E(m, m)$. If the incumbent holds excess capacity, its reaction function is $R^i(x_e/v)$ and the Cournot equilibrium occurs at $E(v, m)$. Depending on the incumbent's choice of capacity, K, the post-entry equilibrium can be any point between A and B on the entrant's reaction function. The point A corresponds to the incumbent's equilibrium output at $E(m, m)$. This is the smallest output that can be sustained by the incumbent as a Cournot equilibrium. The point B corresponds to the incumbent's output at $E(v, m)$ and is the largest output that can be sustained as a Cournot equilibrium. Outputs intermediate between A and B are equilibria for corresponding capacity investment, K. If, given an investment in capacity, K, the equilibrium output that results if a firm entered the market is such that the entrant would not break even, a rational firm would choose to stay out of the market. Thus, prior capacity investment is a way to make an entry deterring limit output 'credible.'

Sunk cost in the Dixit model allow an established firm to maintain a more aggressive response to actual entry than would be possible if costs were not sunk. Dixit also shows the potential entry may encourage an incumbent firm to invest more in irreversible capital. This has the effect of increasing the incumbent's post-entry equilibrium output, while lowering the entrant's post-entry equilibrium output and the post-entry price. In manner similar in spirit to BSM limit pricing, the incumbent invests in capital to deter entry, and, as a result, pre-entry

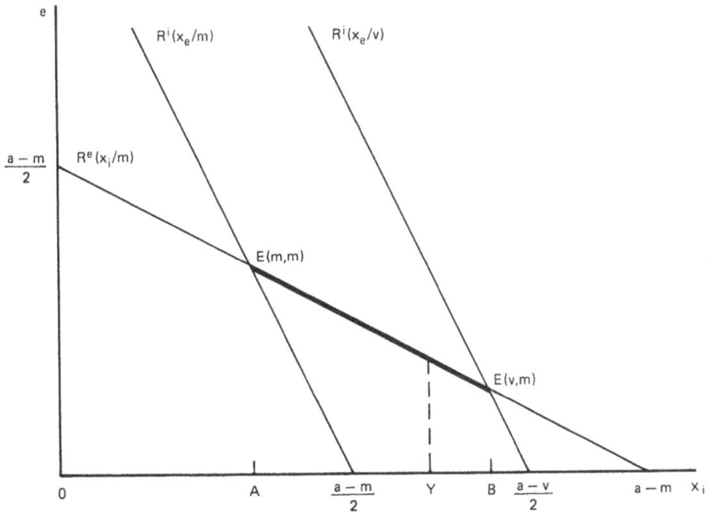

FIGURE 4 Reaction functions and equilibria with capacity investment.

output is higher and pre-entry price is lower than the corresponding monopoly values. The analogy with the classical limit pricing model is even closer because, in Dixit's example, sunk capital allows the incumbent to commit to a fixed output between A and B in Figure 4, and it would be correct for an entrant to assume that the incumbent's output will remain unchanged in response to entry, as assumed in the BSM model.

If capital expenditures were completely reversible, the incumbent firm would have the same cost function as the entrant and the incumbent would be unable to prevent entry by expanding output. Note that the possibility that sunk costs might contribute to the risk of an entry decision (because capital investment might be stranded in an unprofitable industry) is not a factor in the Dixit model. By assumption, there is no uncertainty. Entry occurs if it is profitable and entry is prevented if it is not profitable. Thus, the entrant is not at risk in the Dixit model.

According to the definition of mobility barriers advanced in Section II.D, sunk costs are a potential barrier to *exit* by the established firm, and in the Dixit model this has consequences for the entry decisions of potential rivals. Sunk costs imply that an established firm would tolerate a lower level of profit than it would accept if it were to invest capital in a new venture. The difference between the profit an established firm would earn after entry (after deducting sunk costs) and its profit if it could move capital out of the industry is a measure of the magnitude of the exit barrier. With the technology assumed in the Dixit model, the implication of this exit barrier is that the established firm (with its back to the wall, so to speak) can be an aggressive competitor to a new entrant. Knowing this, the entrant may be better off staying out of the market.

Sunk costs are a Dixit barrier for the established firm that permits the firm to act strategically and capitalize on the entrant's need to operate at a large scale in order to make a profit. Sunk costs are not themselves an entry barrier in the Dixit model, but they allow an established firm to exploit convexities in entrants' costs.[11] Capital investment can be an effective entry deterrent in the Dixit model even if the potential entrant has the same cost function as the incumbent, or even if the entrant has lower cost, because the extent to which costs are sunk plays an important strategic role in permitting the established firm to commit to a level of output that it would maintain if entry were to occur. The established firm's technology with its sunk capital cost is a mechanism by which the firm can sustain the aggressive market share assumptions implicit in the BSM model of limit pricing. In this respect, the Dixit model is a theoretical construction that supports Bain's structural view of economies of scale as a barrier to entry. In the same way, Dixit's model contradicts Stigler's definition of a barrier to entry, which relies on symmetries in the pre-entry costs of established and new firms. Unless one distinguishes costs according to whether or not investment is sunk, the fact is that entry prevention can be achieved in the Dixit model even if the entrant and established firms share the same technology.

Strategic incentives for entry deterrence depend on the correlation between actions which the incumbent can take today and competition in the post-entry game tomorrow. By investing in sunk capital, the incumbent can lower its marginal cost and increase its post-entry

---

[11] Note that the amount of costs that are sunk do not correspond to the height of the barrier to entry as measured by the cost advantage that the entrant must have to successfully enter the industry (see Schmalensee [1981]).

equilibrium output. Actions which make the post-entry game more (less) competitive for the incumbent would increase (decrease) the scope for feasible entry deterrence. The discussion above shows clearly that there are situations where irreversible investment expenditures may allow an incumbent to deter entry, but there is an important caveat to bear in mind. Baumol *et al.* [1982] have argued that fixed costs which give rise to scale economies do not constitute barriers to entry, while sunk costs may. In the Dixit model, for example, the fact that the incumbent cannot recover its capital expenditures, but the entrant can (by not making them), implies that the effective rental rate of capital for the entrant exceeds that of the incumbent. By contrast, fixed costs, which can be completely eliminated in the long run by a total cessation of activity, affect the incumbent and the entrant alike, and can exist in the absence of sunk costs. Baumol *et al.* give the example of the Monday morning garbage collection in a particular neighbourhood. The average cost per residence (including the costs of getting the indivisible truck and driver to the dump) is higher than the marginal cost of serving an additional residence, and so there are increasing returns to scale. However, they argue that a prospective entrant can adopt hit-and-run tactics without cost disadvantage because the truck and driver can be fully employed in other activities by Monday afternoon: there are no sunk costs. Given that an entrant can enter a given market and then exit costly if and when price retaliation occurs, incumbents cannot block entry of a new competitor who is no more efficient. The potential of hit-and-run entry would constrain price to equal average cost in this market.

This argument is not entirely convincing for several reasons. Scale economies and sunk costs are often closely related. Entry into new markets often involves investment in durable plant and long-term labour and supply contracts, and it is rarely the case that these expenditures can be cancelled with no opportunity cost. Even in the case of trash collection, there are additional costs involved in deploying the truck and driver in a different neighbourhood[12] and these would

[12] See Jacquemin [1987], pp. 100–102. Weitzman [1983] argues that if sunk costs are negligible, a technology can be operated in a manner that achieves constant returns to scale. This is accomplished by operating the technology at its most efficient scale, but in sporadic bursts whose durations can be tailored to meet demand. In this way, the desired level of output can be produced at minimum average cost. Note, however, that this argument requires that it be possible to store production long enough to average over the bursts of output.

discourage entry. Even very modest sunk costs would be sufficient to deter entry if the competitive response to entry is sufficiently aggressive. The effectiveness of the entry threat described in Baumol *et al.* relies on the assumption that price would not move quickly relative to the time it takes to enter, earn the profits required to recover any sunk costs, and then leave. If sunk costs are modest, then only a small degree of price rigidity would be necessary to make hit-and-run entry an effective method of market discipline. But there is no assurance that, whatever the level of sunk costs, market prices would be sufficiently rigid to protect a hit-and-run entrant from the rise of an unprofitable entry attempt (see Farrell [1986], Gilbert [1986], and Stiglitz [1987]). Furthermore, whatever the post-entry competition might be, an entrant who anticipates that incumbent firms would act aggressively to maintain market share would deterred from entry if the production technology has increasing returns to scale, regardless of sunk costs. This is the driving principle of the classical BSM model of limit pricing, and Brock and Sheinkman [1981] provide a formalization of the result. They consider the Sylos postulate that quantities would not change after entry and compare the consequences of this assumption to that where potential entrants assume that prices would remain unchanged after entry. Not surprisingly, they find that 'quantity sustainable' equilibria do not have the same socially desirable properties that Baumol *et al.* find for price sustainable equilibria.

The model of limit pricing has attracted criticism not only because of its behaviourial assumptions, but also because it is essentially rather static. Amongst others, Stigler [1968] argued that it may be more desirable to retard the rate of entry rather than to impede entry altogether; Harrod [1952] and Hicks [1954] also pointed to the tradeoff between short run profits and long run losses from entry. Caves and Porter [1977] critized the theory for confining itself to the either/or question of whether a dominant firm will exclude an entrant, and ignoring the more subtle and important issues of the movement into, out of, and among segments of an industry. A related set of problems arises because limit price models focus on competition between insiders and outsiders, neglecting competition between insiders and competition between outsiders. Both types of dynamics consideration and these richer sets of competitive interactions have a major impact on the types of conclusion that are drawn from simple models, and we consider each in turn.

Gilbert and Vives [1986] extend the limit price model of entry prevention to the case of more than one incumbent and a single entrant (the results generalize to more than one potential entrant if entry occurs sequentially — see Vives [1982]). Incumbents act non-cooperatively and each chooses an output taking other firms' outputs as given.

Entry is prevented if the total industry output exceeds the limit output. For the case of linear demand and constant marginal production costs with a fixed entry fee, they show that entry prevention is excessive in the sense that the industry prevents entry at least as much as, and sometimes more than, a perfectly coordinated cartel would. Moreover, there exist multiple equilibria involving entry prevention, and these can co-exist with an equilibrium in which entry is allowed. When equilibria involving entry prevention and accommodation occur simultaneously, the accommodation equilibrium dominates the equilibrium in which entry is allowed. Entry prevention is a public good, and we therefore expect free riding to occur. Yet, there is no tendency to provide too little entry deterrence in the Gilbert and Vives model. The reason is that each incumbent benefits from entry prevention by an amount proportional to its output and this benefit is independent of the number of incumbent firms. In contrast, the benefit of allowing entry to occur falls with the total number of firms in the industry. Thus with more incumbent firms, non-cooperative behaviour tips the balance in favour of entry prevention relative to what a coordinated cartel would do.

Vives [1982] examines how a single incumbent firm would behave in response to several potential entrants who can choose to enter the market sequentially (as in Prescott and Visscher [1978]). He shows that the incumbent firm will choose either to exclude all of the firms or to allow entry by all of the firms who desire to enter the industry. If the number of potential entrants is at least as large as the number of firms that would enter the industry in the absence of entry preventing behaviour, the incumbent should limit price and deter all entrants (see also Omari and Yarrow [1982] and Gilbert [1986]). If entry is deterred, the market structure is, of course, a monopoly; even if entry is allowed, with the assumed production technology in the Vives model, the market would still be very concentrated.

The limit pricing literature describes the incentives for entry prevention and the conditions that are necessary to maintain a level of output sufficient to deter entry. While the classic BSM model of limit pricing shows conditions under which an established firm would prefer to keep out new competition, Dixit's [1981] extension of the limit pricing model shows the range of outputs which an established firm can credibly maintain. In other words, entry prevention may be desirable, but not credible. Gilbert [1986] used data on minimum efficient scale and factor costs in 16 industries to investigate conditions under which entry prevention might be credible by a single established firm. Entry prevention is easier the larger is the minimum efficient scale of entry and the larger is the share of costs that are sunk by an established firm. A large share of sunk costs implies that, *ceteris paribus*, short-run marginal cost when there is excess capacity will be small relative to long-run marginal cost, and this should enable an established firm to maintain a larger output in the face of entry. Gilbert used the share of capital and labour costs as an estimate of sunk costs (the argument for including labour costs is that many labour contracts are difficult to terminate without incurring substantial costs).

Even with the inclusion of labour costs, the share of costs that could be considered as sunk ranged from a low of 23% in petroleum refining to a high of 59% in electric motors. Minimum efficient scale for the 16 industries in the sample varied from about 1% of demand for beer brewing to 23% for turbogenerators. These data allow an estimation of the conditions on demand that would be required to allow a single established firm to maintain an output level large enough to deter entry. From Dixit's [1981] model, this maximum output sustainable against entry increases with (i) the share of sunk costs (assuming the cost function described by equation (1)), (ii) the minimum efficient scale of entry, and (iii) the elasticity of demand. Knowing (i) and (ii), it is possible to estimate how large the elasticity of demand must be for a single established firm to (credibly) prevent entry. For these industries the elasticity of demand must be at least 1.5 (for cement). The minimum elasticity of demand is typically at least 2.0, and is as high as 4.3 (for petroleum refining). A short-run market elasticity in excess of 2.0 is rather high, and this implies that for most of the industries in this sample, a single established firm would have a difficult time maintaining a large enough output to exclude entry of at least one new competitor. Demand is not sufficiently elastic to make the required entry-preventing output of the established firm, even when the share of costs that are sunk is very large.

The elasticity of demand has very different implications for the BSM model of limit pricing and the Dixit model of credible limit pricing. In the BSM model, the established firm is assumed to be able to commit to any level of output. Given the chosen level of output, a less elastic demand makes entry more difficult because the addition of a new firm's output has a larger, negative effect on price (see Waterson [1984]). In a model of credible limit pricing, the limit output must be an equilibrium output of the post-entry game. If demand is not sufficiently elastic, the established firm cannot maintain an equilibrium output large enough to deter entry. If demand and technological conditions are such that a single established firm cannot prevent entry in most industries, limit pricing should address the incentives for oligopolistic firms to prevent entry. Gilbert and Vives [1986] investigated limit pricing by an established oligopoly, but their model assumed that established firms could maintain any desired level of output. Bernheim [1984] considered a model of sequential entry, also under the assumption that established firms could maintain any level of output. Eaton and Ware [1987] examined the consequences of credible commitment in a model with sequential entry. In their model, the number of potential entrants is arbitrarily large (there is free entry), and each firm has a production cost technology similar to that described in equation (1) for which capital investment is irreversible. With free entry, the established firm would maximize profits by deterring the entry of any new rivals. However, conditional on the investments of established firms, the output(s) required to prevent entry may not be sustainable as a post-entry equilibrium, and therefore are not credible entry-preventing outputs. If existing firms do not choose levels of investment and corresponding equilibrium outputs that exceed the limit output, entry occurs until the limit output can be sustained as a sub-game perfect equilibrium. The number of established firms in their model is the smallest number which can credibly deter the entry of an additional firm.[13]

Potential entrants have to evaluate not only the response of incumbent firms to entry, but also the likelihood that future entry will

[13] McLean and Riordan [1989] describe a model that generalizes the problem of credible entry deterrence to the choice of 'accommodating' or 'entry preventing' technologies. They determine how the order of entry into a market affect incentives to choose technologies that, at some cost to established firms, make subsequent entry more difficult. The incentives for entry prevention are also discussed in Waldman [1987].

undermine profits. The threat of excessive entry is particularly severe when entrants act with incomplete information about the decisions of potential competitors. Incomplete information about rival decisions will exist if the time between the decision to enter and actual entry is long and the entry decision is irreversible. Under these conditions, an entrant cannot know if, and how many, other firms will choose to enter. Sherman and Willett [1967] considered the consequences of simultaneous entry and concluded that the possibility of mistakes can discourage entry and lead to a higher limit price. Dixit and Shapiro [1985] explored how the possibility of rectifying entry mistakes through exit or additional entry affects entry incentives. With incomplete information about the actions of other competitors, the entry decision is an investment under conditions of uncertainty. This gives rise to what Richardson [1960] called 'the nomination problem.' There is an optimal number of entrants (most likely greater than one) but no mechanism to determine which of the many potential entrants should be 'nominated' to enter. Farrell [1986b] investigates how non-binding communications (in the absence of side-payments) among potential entrants might avoid the waste from too much or too little entry. He shows that communication, which he calls 'cheap talk', can mitigate, but not necessarily eliminate the nomination problem. His results provide some substance for the type of industry displays, pronouncements and jawboning that often precede a significant entry decision.

We commenced this section by looking at estimates of MEP in search of a structural basis for size-related mobility barriers. Much of the discussion has, however, emphasised the importance played by the strategic behaviour of incumbents, and it is useful to close our discussion by looking at the empirical evidence on the incidence and importance of such behaviour. Limit pricing is to detect because it is triggered by the mere threat of entry and is designed to foreclose entry, since the threat of entry is, in general, difficult to observe. However, when barriers to entry change exogenously and in a manner known by all agents in advance, one can hope to discern some effects. Regulatory changes are an ideal experimental setting, and a clear example of limit pricing can be observed in the UK after the abolition of the solicitor's monopoly on conveyancing which came into effect on 1 May 1987. The regulatory change was known in advance for some time, and prices began to fall as early as 1984, falling by 20% between 1983 and 1986

(Domberger and Sherr, [1987]). Similarly, deregulation in the US and elsewhere has often been accompanied by price cuts in areas where incumbent firms feel threatened by entry (e.g.; Bailey, [1986]). One can also observe some element of limit pricing in response to changes in patent protection, in Xerox's response to entrants using the electrofax process in the early 1960s (e.g.; Blackstone, 1972). Limit pricing is, however, not often easy to distinguish from other price responses to entry, and we shall return to it below in Section V.

The role of strategic investment behaviour and the rise of excess capacity to affect entry and intra-industry competition is rather easier to perceive in a number of cases. For example, Ghemawat [1984] observed an attempt by Du Pont to strategically exclude many of its rivals in the titanium dioxide industry when changes in costs favoured its technology. Modest levels of strategically created excess capacity in the US Aluminum industry were observed by Reynolds [1986], but not of sufficient magnitude to explain observed capacity utilization levels. Lieberman [1987a, 1987b] examined about 40 chemical products industries, observing (particularly in highly concentrated industries) that incumbents increased capacity to reduce the post-entry penetration rate of entrants (but not, it appears, capacity expansion by other incumbents). In this sense, capacity was not used to deter entry so much as to deter mobility. Finally, cross section work by Masson and Shaanan [1986] reveals rather weak evidence that excess capacity was used to deter entry. On the issue of fixed and sunk costs, Kessides [1986] has calculated the degree to which advertising expenditures are sunk in a sample of 266 4-digit US industries between 1972 and 1977, and found that, while entrants appear to perceive a greater likelihood of success in entering highly advertising intensive industries, it nevertheless is the case that advertising appears to give rise to a sunk cost which significantly reduces entry rates. Further, advertising created sunk costs appeared to be more important than those associated with physical capital.

C. Absolute cost advantages

Absolute cost advantages to incumbent firms exist: '... if the prospective unit costs of production of potential entrant firms are generally, and more or less at any common scale of operations, higher than those of established firms . . .' (Bain, [1956], p. 144). Bain defined the absence of absolute cost advantages of an established firm by the following conditions. '. . . For a given product, potential entrant firms should be able to secure just as low a minimal average cost of production after entry as established firms had prior to this entry. This in turn implies that (a) established firms should have no price or other advantages over entrants in purchasing or securing any productive factor (including investible funds); (b) the entry of an added firm should have no perceptible effect on the going level of any factor price; and (c) established firms have no preferred access to productive techniques' (Bain [1956], p. 12). However, not all apparent cost advantages qualify as entry barriers. A cost advantage relative to less efficient potential entrants that is common knowledge to all market participants should not constitute a barrier to entry.[14] While this injects normative considerations into an otherwise positive theory of capital mobility, it would serve no purpose to associate entry barriers exclusively with production inefficiency.[15]

Absolute cost disadvantages refer, at base, to some factor of production that is denied the potential entrant who, but for this omitted factor, would be as efficient as established firms. Of all the possible causes of absolute cost advantages so defined, the first which comes to mind is preferred access to natural resources. Countless possible examples exist. Bain himself associated the ownership of superior ore deposits with 'substantial' barriers to entry in copper, noting that '. . . entry would have to start with the discovery of ore' (p. 154), and 'moderate' barriers to entry in steel where tightness of supply of iron ore (at least in times of active demand) worked to the disadvantage of entrants. Very similar examples have been uncovered in sulphur, nickel (which Mann [1966] judged to have 'high' barriers), mid-Western coal (Comanor, [1966]), retail petrol where certain vertically integrated giants in large measure control supplies (Shaw and Sutton [1976]), and so on.

---

[14] The consequences of an uncertain cost advantage are discussed in Section III. A, where we point out that an established firm may limit price to signal that it is not high cost. Also, note that endogenous cost and advantages may lead to strategic behaviour designed to limit entry. This includes exploiting learning advantages, discussed later in this section.

[15] We do not rule out the possibility that the entry of a less efficient firm may increase welfare, but the association of production inefficiency with entry barriers in the absence of other compounding factors, (such as uncertainty), trivializes the definition problem.

What is not clear in all of this is the role of opportunity costs. A scarce factor of production such as location or special expertise has an opportunity cost of use which must be considered in any decision to continue operations, or to transfer ownership of a scarce factor to a competitor. When this opportunity cost is properly imputed, apparent absolute cost advantages may disappear. Ownership of a scarce factor of production does not, by itself, constitute an absolute cost disadvantage. A scarce factor has an opportunity cost of use which is its market value. The market price of farmland is determined by the marginal productivity of the least productive land that is devoted to agriculture. A farmer that holds title to unusually fertile land does not enjoy an absolute cost advantage relative to other farmers because the market value of the farmer's land is an opportunity cost of farming. The cost difference is a classic Ricardian rent. Although the farmer could exploit the superior quality of his land to price below the cost of other farmers and in that way exclude them from the market, such a strategy would be clearly unprofitable and a theory of entry prevention based upon such unprofitable behaviour would have little normative or descriptive value.

Most discussions of absolute cost difference barriers to entry suggest that control of large ore deposits or key patents is fundamentally different from the control of agricultural land, where most would agree that rents obviate any productivity differences resulting from land quality. Similarly, an ore deposit, whether it is owned by a monopolist or a firm in a relatively unconcentrated industry, has a market value which is the opportunity cost of its use. In this sense, there may be no difference in the cost function of a monopolist or an entrant, and hence no absolute cost difference created by the ore deposit (see also Baumol and Willig [1986]). This view is well articulated by Demsetz [1982] who offers as an example taxi medallions that are issued by a municipality and trade at market-determined prices. The medallions are limited in supply and are required to operate a taxi. In this sense, the medallion requirement impedes the entry of taxi services in this market. Yet the value of the medallion is an opportunity cost of operation for existing as well as potential service providers. It does not favour existing taxis, except to the extent that they may enjoy windfall gains. There is a true barrier to entry in this market, but not in the provision of taxi services. The barrier exists at the level of the municipality, which enjoys an exclusive right to issue medallions. In particular, if costs are properly measured, the medallion requirement would not be a source of supra-normal profits for existing taxis.

An asset that is valued at opportunity cost may nonetheless constitute an absolute cost advantage barrier to entry if the value of the asset is *specific* to its owner, in which case the market value (which is its next best value in use) will understate its worth to the owner. For example, the owner of an ore deposit may have incurred investments in processing equipment that are specific to the ore characteristics of the deposit.[16] A patented technique may be more valuable to its owner because the patent is complementary to other activities of the firm. In these cases, a potential entrant interested in acquiring the asset to effect entry would have to buy the entire firm, because the value of the whole exceeds the sum of its parts. Furthermore, by definition, markets for assets whose values are specific to their owners are thin and, therefore, the market values of these assets are difficult to assess. A pervasive source of asset specificity is the human capital of the management of the firm, which is arguably at least partly specific to the firm's physical assets. Management would be reluctant to part with key assets such as patents or major ore deposits without additional compensation for their loss of earning power. Thus, when the firm-specific nature of scarce factors of production is taken into account, these factors can become barriers to the entry of new competition even if they are valued at market prices.

Patent protection does not prohibit attempts at entry through the purchase of patent rights or entry after their expiry, but it can prevent entry by duplication of the patented technology or product. Thus, Shaw and Shaw [1977] observed substantial increases in entry in polyester fibres after patent protection expired. Bresnahan [1985] observed much the same upon the expiry of Xerox's monopoly in plain paper copiers, and, in a similar vein, the expiration of a number of market sharing agreements in the U.K. metal boxes industry opened up the market to massive entry after 1970 (Prais, [1981] Chapter 18; Shaw and Simpson, [1985]). Mansfield *et al.* [1981] explored imitation costs in several industries, observing that they average about two thirds the

[16] Asset-specific investment again raises the normative question of whether potential entrants are less efficient than the established firm, precisely because they have not made specific investments.

original innovation costs. Patents appear to raise these costs by about 10% in their sample.[17]

As a practical matter, much of the empirical literature on barriers to entry is not concerned with whether absolute cost advantages are truly barriers to entry, but instead whether they allow incumbent firms to earn supra-normal profits. Clearly, the answer to this question depends on whether these assets are carried on the books at their historical costs or at their market values (for a full discussion of this in relation to the use of accounting profits to infer the existence of such barriers, see Edwards *et al.*, [1987]). Consider once again the example of a major ore deposit, and assume that the deposit's value is not specific to its owner so that it is not a barrier to entry. If the deposit is valued at historical acquisition cost, its owner will report a sizable profit that is equal to the difference between its acquisition cost and its current market value. This profit would be reduced if the deposit is carried on the firm's books at its current market value (or replacement cost). Thus, whether or not absolute cost advantages allow firms to earn persistent above-normal profits will depend on, at least in part, the accounting practices of those firms.

Another example of absolute cost barriers arises from information asymmetries which enable incumbents to exploit a superior technology. Bain noted that after the expiration of patent protection in the gypsum industry by Court decree in 1951, continuing problems in the diffusion of knowledge in that industry created a situation where a: '... new firm might be at an appreciable disadvantage for several years' (p. 153). Mann [1966] detected 'high' barriers in ethical drugs, and Freeman [1963] observed that even producers with cost advantages required 15–30 years to challenge patent protected innovation leaders in the plastics industry. A less restrictive patent policy could reduce imitation costs at the risk of providing less incentive for innovation. A classic example of the importance of information symmetries in the creation of absolute cost advantages arises through the need to finance entry attempts under conditions of uncertainty. Morgan *et al.* [1980] identified this as a source of absolute cost disadvantage entry difficulties in the financial leasing industry in the U.K. financial institutions. Brock [1975] observed that, in the early days of the U.S. computer industry, it was generally easy to raise small, or moderate amounts of capital because of investor enthusiasm (the classic example was a firm called Viatron which had a stock market value in 1969 of

$217 million before it made any deliveries, and two years before it folded). By the early 1970's, investor disillusionment, a credit squeeze and IBM's aggressive behaviour all turned capital costs into a significant barrier to entry in the peripherals market. Similarly the early enthusiasm and then sudden collapse of venture capital markets had a major effect on entry into the semiconductor industry (e.g. Levin [1982]). The capital raising problems of entrants are, of course, an example of the more general financial advantages which are widely thought to accrue to large and particularly large, quoted firms (e.g. Prais [1976] and Hay and Morris [1984]). These advantages can arise not only because of rising costs of capital (the problem being that the entrant may have to do quickly what the incumbent was able to over a larger period of time, and so may be forced to borrow more, more quickly), but also the high risk–low collateral combination of borrower characteristics that an entrant presents to lenders may lead to price premia and/or quantity rationing. Systematically assessing the size of financial disadvantages across a wide range of industries is not particularly easy. A preliminary first (but usually also final) step in such calculations is to compute the capital required for efficient entry,[18] but such numbers are not easily converted into interest rate premia, much less into more subtle conditions attached to funds provision. The most that can be said is that the larger the capital requirements, the more likely that even firms established elsewhere will experience difficulty in trying to enter new markets.

Finally, much entry into particular domestic markets occurs through imports of products produced abroad, and it is clear that tariffs and impediments to trade act as a straightforward absolute cost barrier to such entrants. Since the Second War, successive GATT treaties have lowered tariff barriers, but non-tariff barriers to trade of various types

---

[17] A difficulty with absolute cost advantages arising from patents is that, being a clear signal of potential efficiency gains to successful imitators, they may focus the search for information by entrants and so (when there exist numerous ways to do the same thing) facilitate the task of entering on reasonably even competitive terms. This is the natural way to interpret the work on patent-induced rivalry; e.g. Comanor [1964] and Scherer, [1980], Chapter 16.

[18] A common procedure, dating from Comanor and Wilson [1967], is to multiply estimates of MEP by average industry capital intensity. In view of the well known tendency of large firms to be more capital intensive, this is liable to overstate capital requirements, perhaps to an increasing extent in more concentrated industries.

exist. In recent years, there has been a clear shift from the use of generalized safeguards applied on a non-discriminatory basis towards the use of bilateral, industry specific policy-induced barries (like voluntary export restraints and subsidies) in most advanced economies. Tariff and no-tariff intervention has been most common in textiles, clothing, footwear, steel, autos and shipbuilding (e.g. OECD, 1985). Procurement policies by national governments often have the same effect on foreign competitors in advanced sectors like telecommunications, aerospace and others.[19]

Although some types of absolute cost advantages arise fortuitously and some are fixed and exogenous, many interesting exmples exist of obstacles created by the actions of firms, and this raises the possibility that symmetries can be created and exploited to the incumbents advantage. Learning by doing is a classic example of this type of endogenously created cost differential, the premise being that more experience leads to greater efficiency in production (see Lieberman [1984] for an examination of learning advantages in the chemical industry). Experience may be measured by time, cumulative output or some other variable related to job tenure. The important characteristic of experience-related economies is that an established firm enjoys a cost asymmetry relative to new entrants only if the benefits of experience are a private good and do not spread to other industry participants. If this is not so, then the cost asymmetry may be lost or at least severely reduced, and any strategic advantages that may follow from experience would be correspondingly limited.

Depending on the nature of competition in the industry and the rate at which learning-by-doing lowers costs, learning economies need not have the effect of making entry more difficult. Indeed, it is possible that learning economies can make the established firm more willing to allow entry into the industry. Limiting entry requires a firm to price below the average cost of potential entrants. In choosing whether or not to deter entry, the established firm compares its expected profit should entry occur against the profit it would earn by deterring entry. Learning economies, have the effect of increasing incumbent profits

---

19 Peltzman [1965] provides an interesting case study of the effects of legal restrictions on entry rates; see also Spiller and Favaro [1984]. Prais [1981], Chapter 9, discusses the slow response and consequent vulnerability of UK cigarette firms to tax changes.

with or without entry. A large cost advantage can tip the balance in favour of *allowing* entry because the superior efficiency of the established firm makes the firm less vulnerable to competition from a rival producer. Although learning also increases the incumbent's profits when entry is prevented, deterrence requires pricing below the potential entrant's average cost, and profits could be higher if the more efficient firm allows entry to occur (see Mookharjee and Ray [1986]). As in other examples of strategic entry deterrence, the intensity of competition in the post-entry game is crucial to consequences of firm-specific learning for market structure and performance.

The strategic value of experience-related economies depends on the extent to which these economies are firm-specific or spill over to competitors (see Spence [1984] and Kreps and Spence [1984] for a discussion of the consequences of spill-overs in a model with learning; Fundenberg *et al.* [1983] and Harris and Vickers [1985] consider a model of innovation in which experience lowers the expected cost of winning a patent). Much the same conclusions emerge in the case of network economies which refer to complementarities that may exist in consumption or production. In this situation, the value of a good to any one consumer depends on the number of other consumers who purchase the good (telephones are an obvious example.) A simple way in which to model network economies that arise on the demand side of the market is to let price, $P(Q, N)$, depend on Q, total demand, and N, the number of subscribers, with $P_N(Q, N) > 0$. Network economies imply that either willingness-to-pay increases or production cost decreases with the size of the market, and the implications for entry-deterrence parallel the results for markets with experience-related economies (see Katz and Shapiro [1985, 1986]).

Product standardization is a means to appropriate economies that arise as a result of complementarities in production or demand, and hence is closely related to network economies. Adams and Brock [1982] suggest that compatibility standards can be used by an established firm to maintain monopoly power. Matutes and Regibeau [1986a, b] explore this proposition further and find that the opportunity to produce compatible (or incompatible) products can have diverse effects. The opportunity to produce compatible products can lead to higher profits and increased total surplus, although consumers can be worse off with product standardization. Product standardization can lessen a firm's monopoly power by reducing the opportunity to price discriminate among different customers. This can be particularly disadvantageous for a large firm, but it can also enable a firm to forestall entry by making a credible commitment to charge uniform prices across markets that may serve as entry points into the industry.

Production decisions that exploit experience-related economies are one example of strategic behaviour that has consequences for cost symmetries. 'Raising rivals' costs' are another example of this type of endogenously created cost asymmetry. Salop and Scheffman [1983, 1986] explore a general model in which unilateral behaviour by established firms has the effect of raising the costs of potential and actual competitors. The gist of their model follows closely Bain's second condition for the absence of absolute cost advantages: '. . . (b) that the entry of an added firm should have no perceptible effect on the going level of any factor price.' Salop and Scheffman argue that behaviour intended to increase industry costs can benefit established firms (despite increasing their own costs) because it causes rival firms to reduce their output (perhaps to zero). Examples of this phenomenon include efforts to increase union wages, which benefit a firm by making entry by rival firms into the industry more difficult (see Williamson [1968]), strategic behaviour designed to acquire natural resources and deny access to them by rivals (see U.S. v. Aluminum Company of America, 148 F.2d 416 (2d Cir. 1945), and 'sleeping patents' whose value derives from denying access to the technology by competing firms (see Swann [1970], Gilbert [1981] and Gilbert and Newbery [1982]).

It is important to stress that there must exist some exogenous difference between incumbent and entrant if a strategy designed to raise rivals' costs can succeed in deterring entry. If the strategy raises rivals' costs, it is likely to raise the cost of the established firm as well (e.g. increases in union wages). A plausible asymmetry is that the incumbent may be in a position to move first and preempt scarce factors of production (e.g., the acquisition of bauxite ore deposits by Alcoa Corporation alleged in U.S. v. Aluminum Corporation of America). This possibility was considered by Lewis [1983] who found that the case for successful preemption was mixed. While a firm may benefit from the acquisition of scarce inputs, each acquisition increases the price of the input and makes the next acquisition less profitable. Profit-maximizing behaviour can lead the firm to stop short of acquiring all of the inputs necessary to exclude entry.

Related to strategies that raise rivals' costs are agreements among established firms and/or customers that limit access by actual or potential competitors to particular markets.[20] Aghion and Bolton [1986] provide an interesting example of an exclusionary practice that deters entry. In their model, an established firm can enter into long-term contracts with customers that specify prices conditional on the entry of a competitor. Potential rivals are disadvantaged by not being able to sign such contracts, and are limited to spot price offers for their products. Aghion and Bolton show that there exist contracts that exclude entry in circumstances where, absent such contracts, entry would have occurred. This exclusionary practice has the simple form of a 'take-or-pay' contract, and if customers switch to a rival supplier, they must pay the incumbent firm a fee. What is interesting is that it is in the customers interests to enter into these agreements if the contract allocates to consumers some of the benefits from entry prevention. In Aghion and Bolton's example, entry-prevention minimizes production costs, and therefore it is not surprising that there exists a contract between firms and customers that excludes entry. More generally, it can be shown that entry-preventing contracts exist between the incumbent and customers that exclude entry when entry would be efficient. This arises because the potential entrant is excluded from the contract negotiations and so the scope for efficient bargaining is limited.

D. Product differentiation

Advantages to incumbent firms associated with barriers created by product differentiation refer to: '. . . buyers' preferences for one of the same variety of very similar substitute products . . . and also to the fact that different buyers have different product allegiances or preference patterns, so that the preferences in question do not result in some universally agreed upon system of grading or rating of the competing products' (Bain, [1956], p. 114). Such effects can be propagated by differences in design, quality, or sales promotion, with the effect that

[20] Strategies that limit the size of a rival's market increase the rival firm's average costs if the rival's production technology has increasing returns to scale. In this sense, demand-reducing strategies can be similar in effect to cost-increasing strategies.

each '. . . individual seller gains some jurisdiction over his price' (p. 114).

While clearly '. . . a preference, transitory or permanent, for some or all established products as compared to new entrant products' (Bain, [1956], p. 114) makes it unlikely, *ceteris paribus*, that entrants will be able to replicate post-entry the pre-entry price-cost margins enjoyed by incumbents without expending resources to develop their own consumer loyalties, the interesting question is how such a state of affairs could come to pass in a way that is advantageous to early entrants in a market. Evidently, to make reasonable choices amongst 'experience goods' (those which the consumer must consume in order to usefully evaluate; see Nelson [1970]), the consumer must acquire information. However, these search costs are sunk costs, and so a prior investment with one particular brand will weaken consumer's interest in other new brands which arrive later on the market (this is briefly discussed by Bain [1956] p. 116; see also Comanor and Wilson [1974], (Chapters 3–4), and the model developed by Schmalensee [1981]). Even with 'search goods' whose worth can be established prior to purchase or experience goods purchased frequently, it may be costly for consumers to re-evaluate their consumption programme with the arrival of new information, and the consequent routinization of purchasing decisions by consumers forces late coming entrants to incur 'switching costs' in their efforts to achieve market penetration.

Thus, entrants must persuade consumers already settled in their ways to collect information, compare products with different specifications and then to re-evaluate their purchasing habits. The incumbent might avoid such switching costs simply because it was first on to the market, but these information asymmetries can cut both ways. The first producer of a new product or service has to prove its worth to sceptical consumers; subsequent producers have the disadvantage of contending with the reputation of an established firm, but may have the advantage of a better-informed customer base.[21]

Switching costs represent a consumer disutility from changing

[21] Farrell [1986a] notes that new entrants may have a tougher time convincing customers that they will deliver comparable quality. In Farrell's model, competition lowers the future benefits from investments in quality. If consumers believe that new entrants do not have sufficient incentives to invest in high quality, they may be reluctant to experiment with their products. This result depends on the value of future profits to the entrant, and on the firm's ability to warrant the quality of its goods.

brands which may result from direct costs of switching or simply from a distaste for sampling other brands. They are a source of diseconomies of scope in consumption because, with switching costs, a customer is better off continuing to purchase from the original supplier even though another supplier offers the same product at a slightly lower price. A firm that sells Q units to customers each of which has a switching cost, f, has a demand curve as in Figure 5. Ignoring possibilities for price discrimination, the firm has a choice of pricing high to exploit existing customers (e.g. selling to its old customers at a price P_o), or pricing low to attract and 'lock-in' customers (e.g. selling to both old and new at a price P_n). The cost of switching is an obvious source of monopoly power to established suppliers (see Schmalensee [1981] and Klemperer [1986]). However, while switching costs favour an established supplier, their implications for industry structure are far from obvious. Customer expectations of how firms will react to price competition are crucial to the effects of switching costs. If customers of established firms believe that equilibrium prices will be the same for all firms and that price changes will occur rapidly, they will chose to remain with their original suppliers even if switching costs are small. This gives established firms a sure hold over their customer base. Alternatively, customers may act in the spirit of Nash and evaluate

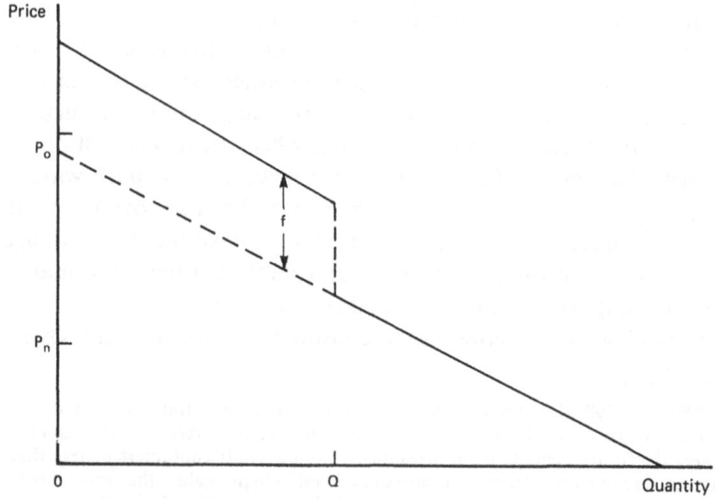

FIGURE 5 Demand with switching costs.

competitive price offers assuming other prices will not change. In this case, an established firm's grip on its old customers may be less secure.

Farrell and Shapiro [1986] investigate an overlapping-generations model of competition with switching costs in which either a new supplier or the established supplier acts as a Stackelberg price leader and there is no opportunity for price discrimination. Both firms have identical and constant marginal costs. When the entrant moves first and sets a price, p, the incumbent can either (a) sell to only its old customers at a price $p+f$ (or slightly below) or (b) compete for all customers by setting a price slightly below p. They show that there is a unique equilibrium in which the entrant serves only new customers at a price p and the established supplier serves only old customers at a price $p+f$. The incumbent never competes for the new customers. The reason is that the new customers are equally valuable to the incumbent and the rival, but the incumbent has an incentive to price higher and keep its old customers. Allowing for economies of scale, Farrell and Shapiro show that a customer base with switching costs can lead an established firm to allow entry when entry prevention would be more efficient. This result parallels the example with learning. In the learning case, it would be efficient for the firm with lower costs to price low and deter entry. But, the firm may choose to exploit its low cost by pricing high and allowing entry. Similarly, the firm with a customer base could price low and prevent entry or price high, keep its old customers, and allow entry to occur. If economies of scale are not too great, the latter course of action is the best strategy.[22]

This discussion of the source of product differentiation advantages suggests that an obvious way to examine whether they exist is to examine the experience of pioneering brands in markets that experience subsequent entry. Urban *et al.* [1984] examined 129 frequently purchased consumer brands in 12 US markets, and related the share of nth movers relative to first movers to the order of entry, entry lags, relative advertising and brand positioning. The order of entry turned

---

22 These results follow under the assumption that the entrant acts as a Stackelberg price leader. If the incumbent is the price leader, there is a unique equilibrium with a single price charged by both firms (the same for both new and old customers). Old customers strictly prefer to buy from their old firm, while new customers are indifferent. Profits for both firms are higher when the incumbent is the price leader, but curiously the entrant benefits even more in this instance. There is a 'second-mover advantage' in the game with the incumbent as the price leader.

out to be positively correlated with relative shares. The second brand in the market had a share less than 75% of the pioneer on average, the third about 66%, the fourth about 50% and so on, all for the same given levels of advertising. Put another way, if the second brand wanted to achieve the same share as the pioneer, it would need to have done nearly 3.4 times the volume of advertising as the pioneer. Numerous case studies (particularly of the pharmaceutical industry) also suggest that early movers do, in fact, appear able to sustain their market positions against later 'me-too' entrants. Grabowski and Vernon [1982], for example, observed that heavy brand promotion in the US pharmaceutical industry tended to protect pioneering firms from entry even long after patents expired (see also Bond and Lean [1977]). A case study of the Canadian drug industry by Gorecki [1986] found that late entrants tended to succeed in capturing a decent market share only in regional markets where pharmacists were allowed to select lower priced brands. However, this relatively successful market penetration seems to have been won at the cost of having to sell late arriving brands at something of a discount relative to the incumbent pre-entry (and, in fact, often relative to the incumbent post-entry), suggesting that a barrier exists.

Advertising and market expenditures may serve to impede entry if there's an asymmetry in the way that firms' advertising expenditures affect their demands (e.g. Schmalensee [1974]). Advertising also may increase product differentiation and exacerbate the effects of scale economies on the profitability of entry. When combined with a scale-related barrier to entry, firms might find it profitable to enhance product differentiation in order to exploit the benefits of scale. Spence [1980] shows how advertising expenditures can influence the optimal scale of production by affecting both the cost of operation and the revenues that can be collected at a particular level of output.

Dixit [1979] employs a simple model to trace the interactions between economies of scale, the extent of product differentiation, and the scope for entry deterrence. There is an established firm (firm 1) and a potential entrant (firm 2), with demands of the form

$$p_1 = a_1 - b_1 x_1 - c x_2 \tag{1}$$

$$p_2 = a_2 - b_2 x_2 - c x_1 \tag{2}$$

with a_1, $b_1 > 0$ and $c < (b_1 b_2)^2$. The products are substitutes if $c > 0$. Each firm has a cost function $C_i = m x_i + F$. For simplicity we assume that the established firm can commit pre-entry to an output level that it will produce post-entry and so acts as a Stackelberg leader. The limit output in this model is

$$Y = [a_2 - m - 2(b_2F)^{1/2}]/c. \tag{3}$$

The extent of production differentiation affects all of the parameters of demand for the two brands. Dixit calls particular attention to the effects on the intercepts of the inverse demand functions (a_i) and the cross-product term (c). An increase in advertising and marketing expenditures that enhances brand 1 at the expense of brand 2 may increase a_1 relative to a_2 and decrease c. The intercept (a) effect measures an increased willingness to pay for brand 1 relative to brand 2 at every level of output; the decrease in the cross-product term (c) lowers the cross-elasticity of demand for the two brands (they become poorer substitutes).

Ignoring the cost of product differentiation, the incentive for demand-enhancing activities can be examined by comparing profits earned when entry occurs to the profits earned at the limit output. A decrease in a_2 lowers the limit output, while a decrease in c has the opposite effect. The a effect increases the profit earned when entry is prevented, and the c effect goes the other way as entry prevention is more difficult when products are poorer substitutes. (Products must be substitutes in order for the output of one product to adversely affect the profits earned by the other products; if the products are independent, limit pricing is useless.) Dixit concludes that 'a greater absolute advantage in demand (or cost) for established firms makes entry harder, but lower cross-price effects with potential entrants make entry easier. This suggests that industrial organization economists should keep these two aspects distinct, instead of lumping them together into one vague concept of product differentiation as they usually do.' (p. 32)

Attempts to measure product differentiation barriers often start by equating barriers due to product differentiation with barriers due to advertising, at least partly because many scholars see advertising as the principal cause of product differentiation barriers. Comanor and Wilson are, perhaps, the most prominent advocates of this approach. Arguing that advertising expenditures: '. . . are both a symptom and a source of differentiation . . .' [1967], p. 423), they identified absolute cost, economies of scale, and capital requirements sources of entry barriers due to advertising (pp. 425–6; see also their 1974 book and

1979 survey). In practice, they used advertising-sales ratios to measure absolute cost advantages, and advertising per firm to pick up economies of scale and capital requirements effects. Their initial finding of significant positive correlation between advertising intensity and profitability has been replicated in countless studies, and has generally been interpreted as establishing the importance of this source of entry barrier.[23]

There are, however, a number of reasons to avoid equating product differentiation with advertising and to think that advertising expenditures may be a fairly poor way to measure the height of barriers associated with product differentiation. The major objections arise because advertising is not a structural characteristic of markets. Rather, it is one of the methods by which incumbents compete against each other in certain types of markets, and firm by firm or industry by industry variations in advertising intensity reflect the joint selection of price and non-price strategies by rivals (e.g. Dorfman and Steiner [1954]). The basic structural determinants of the choice of advertising levels are consumer preferences, consumer informativeness, and the technology of production and of information transmission (e.g. Butters [1976], esp. p. 395), and, clearly, it is in these structural conditions that the source of product differentiation barriers lies. One immediate implication of this observation is that, even if advertising played no role in entry, it may still be correlated with profitability

[23] One source of controversy generated by these empirical results concerns the expensing of advertising and whether one should try to account for its capital investment nature (Block [1974]; Ayanian [1975]; Weiss [1968]; Demsetz [1979]; Comanor and Wilson [1974] Chapter 8; Siegfried and Weiss [1974]. Problems seem to have arisen only when implausibly low values of the depreciation rate are used (e.g. Scherer [1980], p. 286 or Comanor and Wilson [1979], pp. 462–7). Attempting to measure the stock of goodwill rather than current advertising also seems less pressing now than when it was initially advocated, partly because of frequent observations of high depreciation rules associated with advertising (e.g. Clarke [1976]). Much finer, more subtle correlations between advertising and profitability have been found by considering the types and media mix of advertising (e.g. Porter [1976]), the structure and profit differentiating activities of retailers (e.g. Porter [1974]), the type of market and hence the role advertising plays in informing or persuading consumers (e.g. Boyer [1974]), who distinguishes 'good will' from 'informative' advertising), the difference between firm and aggregate industry advertising (the latter allegedly capturing entry barriers — see Vernon and Nourse [1973]), the effect of possible simultaneous equations bias (Comanor and Wilson [1974], 1953–64; Strickland and Weiss [1976]; Geroski [1982]; Martin [1979], and so on. More general discussions of these issues can be found in Schmalensee [1972], Cowling *et al.* [1975], and Ferguson [1974].

simply because of the manner in which it is determined (e.g. Schmalensee [1976]; Needham [1976]). Hence, such correlations cannot be read as necessarily reflecting entry difficulties.[24]

In fact, the role of advertising in affecting entry is more subtle than its use as a proxy for product differentiation suggests. Consider the following simple model in which an incumbent firm chooses a price, p_i and an advertising level A_i. A new firm that enters the industry would earn

$$\Pi_e = p_e x_e(p_e, p_i, A_e, A_i) - C_e(x_e, A_e) \tag{4}$$

if it chose price p_e and advertising A_e, producing X_e in consequence. For any particular level of advertising by the incumbent, it is obvious that the entrant is better off when it can advertise, and, in this sense, advertising serves the pro-competitive function of making a new brand known to consumers. To the extent that advertising increases a firm's perceived elasticity of demand, it can lead to lower equilibrium prices. A classic demonstration of this effect was reported by Benham [1972] who noticed that in states where opticians were allowed to advertise, competition was more vigorous and prices were lower than in states where they were not. This said, when incumbents advertise entrants are also forced to do so, and this additional cost of entry can create problems for some putative entrants (see Cubbin [1981]).

Differential access to capital to finance an advertising campaign, economies of scale in advertising, and so on all generate anti-competitive effects associated with advertising. Advertising expenditures increase the cost of producing a particular level of output, but, as Spence [1980] has noted, it is net revenue and not cost that is the relevant quantity with product differentiation. Advertising facilitates entry if its revenue-enhancing effects compensate for its higher costs. If

---

[24] Reinforcing this ambiguity in interpreting the effect of advertising on profits are the somewhat varied and conflicting empirical results reported in the literature on market share instability. Telser [1964] discovered that market shares were noticeably less stable in more advertising intensive industries; Havrileski & Barth [1969] found shares to be generally stable in cigarettes, one of the most heavily advertised sectors; Caves & Porter [1978] found that advertising reduced instability (but not significantly) and product R&D raised it (significantly); and Meisel [1981] found that the frequent introduction of new brands raised instability. For a survey which discusses, *inter alia*, the effect of advertising on the level of market concentration, see Curry and George, [1983]. The link between either set of correlations and the height of entry barriers due to product differentiation is no more direct than that illuminated by advertising-profits correlations.

the opposite is true, advertising can make entry more difficult. Both sets of effects were observed by Geroski and Murfin [1987a, 1987b] in a study of entry into the UK Car Market. Firms—including entrants—who were able to capture a large advertising share were able to enter and expand in the market, but entry gradually became more difficult as the costs of capturing a large share rose. These costs did, in fact, rise as early entrants and incumbents embarked on a post-entry advertising war that, in the end, disadvantaged later entrants. Thus, advertising by entrants can facilitate entry, but at a cost which depends, *inter alia*, on the advertising of incumbents.

Even if advertising has adverse consequences on the profitability of entry by new competitors, this does not imply that advertising has *strategic* value as an entry deterrent. In order to qualify as a strategic variable, an established firm must be able to manipulate its advertising program prior to entry with positive consequences for profits earned in the post-entry period. If an established firm cannot use advertising to create lasting demand asymmetries or otherwise affect consumer or rival producer behaviour in post-entry periods, advertising has no particular strategic value as an entry deterrent. This point was made by Schmalensee [1974] in a model where advertising expenditures contribute to a firm's goodwill (its present value profits), but have no influence on long-run behaviour after entry can occur. Furthermore, even if advertising can be used as a strategic variable, it need not be used to prevent entry. Fudenberg and Tirole [1984] offer an example where advertising does not prevent entry, but, by making demand less elastic, results in higher prices for both established firms and new competitors. There are numerous other factors which can create a preference for established products relative to those of an entrant. One obvious source of asymmetry lies in the design and variety of products. A naturally limited product space may be pre-empted by incumbents to restrict the demand attainable by entrants for a given outlay, and the necessity to match product specifications involving high fixed costs may make revenue generation very costly for small or moderate scale entry. Examples of the former are suggested by the US ready-to-eat breakfast cereal market (see Schmalensee [1978]) and the UK fertilizer industry (Shaw [1982]). In the breakfast cereal market, economies of scale are small (3–5% of the market), the technology is simple and the capital requirements for constructing an efficient scale plant are modest. Nevertheless, despite consistently high profits from 1950 to the early 1970s, no entry occurred. Part of the reason for this undoubtedly has to do with the need for entrants to advertise heavily to match the promotional activities of incumbents, but the fact that the number of brands tripled over the period suggests that a systematic policy of brand proliferation by incumbents also have made entry difficult. In terms of simple geographical space packing, the cement industry provides an example of the same type of barrier (Scherer [1980] p. 256). Indeed, geographical space provides the most reliable example of this type of phenomena, since 'product spaces' are poorly defined and therefore are rather difficult to crowd (witness the quite unexpected growth of a natural cereals submarket in the ready-to-eat market). Automobile styling costs are a classic example of an inflation of relatively fixed marketing costs which work to the disadvantage of relatively small scale producers (e.g. Fisher *et al.* [1962], or White [1977]).

Finally, another source of asymmetry arises when the provision of a good requires a basic interaction between buyers and the seller, such as the provision of pre-or post-sale services. Bain ([1956], appendix D) calculated that in the steel industry, personal sales representation, assisting with technical services plus special treatment in the matter of delivery dates created a 'slight' entry barrier necessitating an expenditure for one or two years of about 2% (relative to price) more by entrants trying to break into this market. Not unrelated to direct buyer-seller interaction is the role of retail and wholesale networks, and access to them by entrants. The 'solus' system of long term contracting between garages and suppliers of retail petrol in the UK caused the many entrants into this industry in the 1960s to set up their own outlets in an already geographically crowed space and that, no doubt, created a mild disadvantage ([Shaw], 1974). Tied houses also block the entry by new brewers in the UK beer industry (e.g. Shaw and Sutton [1976]). Bain (appendix D) found 'moderate' barriers (a 2.5–5% higher price net of selling cost) for leaders in the replacement market for rubber types largely as the result of such control, and entrants into the typewriter market were estimated as needing 5–10 years to build up competitive repair and maintenance services. Dealer systems also appeared important, and as one of several causes of problems in another industry with 'great' entry barriers, namely automobiles.

E. A summing-up

It would seem natural to conclude from the foregoing that there are a wide range of factors which can serve as barriers to mobility. Although the various structural conditions discussed above do not always necessarily give rise to barriers, there appears to be much scope for strategic activity by incumbents to exploit such conditions to their own advantage. Taken together, the obstacles to entry and intra-industry mobility seem to be many and their impact on entrants appear, at first sight, to be impressive. However, this said, one must also add that there are good reasons to resit drawing this conclusion, and most of them are bound up with the way that barriers have been measured in practice.

As noted in Section II, there are several different definitions of barriers to mobility in the literature. The empirical work subsequent to Bain's own painstaking measurement exercise has generally tried to follow his procedures. However, in practice, this has often amounted to comparing actually observed entrants with incumbents, or has involved rather simple counter-factual constructions based on observations of incumbents' activities. The implicit or explicit use of incumbent's current activities as 'the best possible under the circumstances' creates an upward bias in measuring barriers since it neglects the opportunity that entrants may have to do better than incumbents. Consider, for example, the case of product differentiation. Since the definition of a product is at least as elastic as the collective imagination of all currently successful producers, there always exists the possibility that a little creativity can successfully engineer a leap into the (apparently) safest of markets. For example, it is difficult to understand why Smiths could not have developed the new retail outlets and the new material sales orientation that Golden Wonder used to enter the seemingly safe UK Potato Crisp industry in the early 1960s, nor why it took such a shock to galvanize Smiths into finally developing new flavours for crisps (Bevan [1974]). Similarly, the entry of Rolls Razor into the UK domestic washing machines market in 1958, using a marketing strategy concentrating on price cutting and by-passing traditional retail outlets, was '... founded on the inadequacies of established firms ...' (Shaw and Sutton [1976], p. 51). Its short life in the industry seems to have transformed the market in terms of the specification and marketing of goods, a transformation that ought to have been well within the capabilities of incumbents absent entry. The spectacular success it enjoyed and the rather lagged response (at least initially) of incumbents underlay the innovative nature of its entry challenge, and demonstrates how creative imagination can simply sweep past what appear, pre-entry, to have been moderate product differentiation barriers. One does not have to read from these examples: '. . . a warning against too ready an acceptance of product differentiation as a serious barrier to entry . . .' (Shaw and Sutton, p. 52); it is enough to recognize the particularly hazardous nature of the necessary counterfactual construction involved in measuring barriers due to product differentiation.

The rather large number of definitions of barriers to entry that exist in the literature give rise to a second observation, namely that the existence of a wide range of factors which may make entry difficult does not imply that all of these factors reduce efficiency, or require policy attention. There are circumstances in which 'too much' entry can occur, and barriers which prevent such outcomes are not necessarily bad. Indeed, the raw data discussed in Section 1 gave rise to a clear impression that many entrants fail, or, if they succeed, do so only at the expense of very small sized incumbents. The extremely high turnover rates that one observes in many industries may, perhaps, be avoidable, and tolerating some barriers may reduce the waste that seems to be involved in this process.

The third observation is that the time importance of entry barriers depends on the used to measure entry and exit. As noted in the Introduction, barriers can be thought of as costs of adjustment which the entrant must incur to successfully penetrate into the market. They are not necessarily permanent obstacles, and to think of them in that way may exaggerate their importance. In the short run, any given barrier will present a much more imposing set of obstacles to an entrant than it will when viewed over the medium to long run and after the entrant has had a chance to design and implement a strategy to deal with its disadvantage. Given time and finance, many apparently imposing obstacles can be circumvented by a clever entrant and the interesting question that arises is what it is that makes so many entrants apparently unequal to the task.

Thus, one must take care in interpreting the evidence that we have discussed above. It is almost certainly the case that the various structural conditions which can give rise to barriers are ubiquitous;

equally certainly, one can overstate their importance. Aside from the measurement problems discussed above, it is also the case that what is often of importance is the extent to which structural factors are strategically exploited by incumbents to deter entry. Economies of scale *per se* do not block entry, but, rather, it is the threat of large price cuts attendant upon attempted entry at MEP scale which discourages entrants. Similarly, it is almost certainly the case that advertising by an entrant will facilitate its attempt at entry, but the important issue is how costly the necessary advertising will be, a calculation which must depend on the advertising response of incumbents. In evaluating the various structural determinants of entry, then, one ought also to explore the incidence of various types of strategic entry behaviour.

Aside from various case studies, there is little in the way of systematic evidence on the incidence of strategic entry deterrence. Four surveys, however, have produced evidence to suggest that it occurs less frequently than one might imagine. Biggadike [1976] asked a sample of 35 US entrants about their perceptions of the reaction to their entry attempts. 46% perceived no response from incumbents whatsoever, and, of the range of competitive weapons available (price, excess capacity, and so on), that which was most often used was an increase in marketing expenditures. Yip [1982] looked at 36 entrants in the US and found no response to entry by acquisition and only a response incidence of about 20% (at most) to direct entry. Smiley [1988] sent a questionnaire to 293 US firms and discovered that learning advantages, the installation of excess capacity and limit pricing were either never used or were used infrequently by more than 75% of the firms; by contrast, advertising and patent policy were used more than infrequently by about 60% of the firms. Finally, Cubbin and Domberger [1988] studied entry into 42 advertising intensive UK industries, perceiving no response by 60% of the firms in their sample.

The evidence from these four sources can be read in different ways. Structural factors may present such a large obstacle to entrants that strategic activity to deter entry attempts may be unnecessary. Alternatively, strategic behaviour may not be used because it is unlikely to have a large enough impact to ward off entry attempt. Another possibility is that once entry occurs, it is rational for established firms to accommodate entry rather than engage in aggressive behaviour to discourage the growth of new firms.[25] The survey results are subject to serious sample bias because some of the evidence was collected only from interviews with *successful* entrants. These firms may have been successful because they brought innovative technology or management to the industry or because established firms failed to take advantage of structural barriers that would have prevented new competition. Excluded from the survey populations were firms that were unsuccessful entrants and firms that chose not to enter an industry because they did not expect to succeed. Note also that the survey findings of 'no response' to entry can mean many different things. In the case of production, 'no response' can be consistent with established firms maintaining their pre-entry levels of output, which is assumed in the BSM model of limit pricing. If entry required a significant scale of operation, the failure of established firms to respond to entry by changing output results in a lower price. This form of 'no response' amounts to an entry deterrent. Finally, the data on entry and the evidence on the stability of the shares of established market leaders make it difficult to avoid the impression that incumbents do not often need to assist entrants in making a rapid exit from the market. The life of most entrants is likely to be 'nasty, brutish and short' even when incumbents treat them with benign neglect, and that, of course, suggests that benign neglect often may be an optimal policy for incumbents to adopt.

IV. EXIT BARRIERS AND ASSET SPECIFICITY

Exit of a firm from an industry is a special case of capital mobility, and barriers to exit can be defined in a way that is symmetrical to the definition of entry barriers. Applying the definition of entry barriers developed by Bain to the problem of exit, an exit barrier exists if established sellers earn profits that are less than the profits that can be earned by firms that have not entered the industry. A proxy for the latter is a normal return on investment. A generalization of Stigler's measure of entry barriers would measure an exit barrier by a cost that a firm must bear in order to leave a market, but is not borne by firms that

[25] Note that in this respect the evidence from these four sources is not consistent with the findings of Lieberman (1987a), who reports that new investment by established firms in concentrated industries is positively correlated with the entry of new competitors.

are not yet established in the market (or by established firms that have not chosen to leave the market). Applying the theory of mobility barriers, a barrier to exit exists if a firm could move its capital into another market and achieve a higher return than it is earning in its present market. These definitions can be extended to introduce the welfare consequences of exit, as von Weizsacker has done for the case of entry barriers.

As in the case of barriers to entry, whether a particular structural condition of a market contributes to a barrier to exit generally will depend on the definition of the exit barrier that is employed. A straightforward candidate for a barrier to exit is a fee imposed through a supply contract or a penalty assessed by a regulatory body that would be triggered if a firm were to exit a market. Sunk costs may contribute to an exit barrier (under the definition of Bain) and the theory of mobility barriers because with sunk costs a firm may tolerate a lower return than would be acceptable if the firm were to invest in a new market where costs are not yet sunk. However, sunk costs would not appear to constitute a barrier to exit under the generalization of Stigler's definition.

Exit costs can magnify the consequences of competition in a declining market. Consider a classic war of attrition (see, e.g. Ghemawat and Nalebuff [1985], Fudenberg and Tirole [1986]). In a war of attrition, one or more firms have to leave a declining market, but there is no mechanism to choose which firm must go. Suppose that there are two firms in a market which has shrunk to the point where only one firm can operate profitably. Even with no costs of exit, neither firm may be satisfied to leave the market, which would then be profitable for the remaining firm. This can lead to ruinous competition as each firm becomes determined to be the last to go. The presence of exit costs can reinforce this self-destructive tendency. Only the absence of both exit and entry costs would resolve the war of attrition, because then neither firm would tolerate negative earnings if it could leave and return to the market at will.

Barriers to exit can affect entry in two ways. They affect the risk of an entry decision by adding to the cost that an entrant would have to bear if events subsequent to entry prevent it from leaving the market. Barriers to exit also may affect entry by influencing the competitive incentives of established firms. If barriers to exit are large, established firms may be counted upon to remain as competitors if entry occurs, and may act as if their backs are against the wall. As we have seen, the Dixit model of credible entry deterrence is a particular example of the effect on competition of a potential barrier to exit (sunk costs). In the Dixit model, sunk costs affect the competitive incentives of the established firm, making the firm a more formidable competitor than it would be if its capital were not sunk.

The incentive effects of barriers to exit are particularly important for competition in markets where firms produce several products that are close substitutes . . . Judd [1985] demonstrated that even the presence of sunk costs may be insufficient to deter entry in such markets. Entry into one of the product markets of a multiproduct firm results in price erosion that lowers profits in the market that was challenged and in the markets for substitute goods. A multiproduct firm can protect the profits earned on its substitute goods by abandoning the particular market that was challenged by an entrant. This provides a potential window of opportunity for entry by a single-product firm. The entrant can anticipate that a multiproduct firm would want to protect its profits from substitute products. In effect, the incentive effects are the opposite of those in Dixit [1981]. The established firm's multiple products make the firm a less formidable competitor in a single market, and this invites entry by a single-product firm. Judd's model is a good example of the general proposition advanced by Fudenberg and Tirole [1984] and Bulow *et al.* [1985] that strategic behaviour in a particular market is shaped by the competitive effects in related markets.

Judd's model shows that sunk costs may not act as a barrier to entry into multiproduct industries. Indeed, Judd argues that sunk costs should have no effect on the decision of an established multiproduct firm to abandon a particular product. The abandonment decision depends on a comparison of the profits that an established firm would earn after entry when the firm keeps its original product portfolio with the profits that the firm would earn if it dropped the challenged product. Sunk costs are irrelevant to this comparison. However, a multiproduct firm would be less inclined to abandon a challenged product if abandonment incurred additional costs. Thus, the presence of exit costs as defined by Stigler would make entry more difficult in the Judd model of multiproduct firms.

Exit costs may arise when a firm's assets are specific to a production in progress (e.g. Caves and Porter [1976]). An asset is specific to a particular economic activity if the value of its services in this activity strictly exceeds its value in an alternative use. The difference in value relative to the next best use is a measure of the cost of exit. Williamson [1975, 1985] uses the concept of asset specificity to develop a theory of market and institutional structure, and it is clear that asset specificity is at the heart of Bain's absolute cost advantage and product differentiation barriers to entry. The owner of a unique asset should value the asset at its opportunity cost, which is determined by the market. If an asset is specific, its opportunity cost is less than its value in its best use and there is an absolute cost advantage. Asset specificity can take varied and subtle forms. The company may have technological skills, patents, marketing experience, or a reputation for service that are complementary to the firm's other physical or human capital, and increase the value of its capital relative to its opportunity cost. Managers have human capital that is complementary to the firm's assets, and may therefore value the firm (and their own marginal products) at levels that exceed their opportunity costs. Caves and Porter [1976] suggest that managers' specific human capital is one reason why firms appear to cling to apparently unprofitable activities. Managerial asset specificity impedes the mobility of capital out of struggling industries. Investments in advertising and marketing are often also asset specific.

Asset specificity is a powerful concept, but it has limitations as an explanation of the determinants of entry barriers. Although asset specificity may be the ultimate barrier to capital mobility, the identification of the relevant specific asset(s) may prove too difficult to make the concept empirically useful in all situations. Consider the role of sunk costs in the Dixit model of entry deterrence. Sunk costs allow an established firm to commit itself to producing an output large enough to deter entry. Sunk costs are asset specific, and this example of entry deterrence appears to be another case where asset specificity is at the heart of barriers to entry and exit. But is it? Entry deterrence is feasible because the incumbent firm has a mechanism which enables it to commit to an output level that makes entry unprofitable. In the Dixit model, this mechanism is sunk costs (specific assets). But any mechanism that allows the incumbent firm to commit to an output at least as large as the limit output will do. The incumbent might be able to persuade customers to sign long term supply contracts and so shift its reaction function to the right by an amount large enough to deter entry. One might argue that the entrant would want to do this too, and would be willing to sell these contracts at a price equal to its value to the entrant — unless the ability to persuade consumers to sign contracts is an asset whose value is specific to the established firm. This logic seems correct, but also tautological. In practice, identifying the incumbent's specific asset may be more difficult than identifying the incumbent's ability to commit to a limit output as the mechanism for entry deterrence.

V. DYNAMIC LIMIT PRICING AND MODELS OF SEQUENTIAL COMPETITION

There is a fine difference between policies implemented pre-entry which are designed to block entry, and those which may be used post-entry to cause exit or, at least, to limit the market penetration of entrants. For example, a limit pricing strategy involves price cutting prior to entry to deter putative competitors, while predatory pricing strategies may be used post-entry to drive out new competitors. Somewhere in between these two strategies is what has come to be called 'entry regulation'. Although it is a strategy designed to limit the rate at which entrants penetrate into a market, this type of strategy is also a useful way to think about the two options open to incumbents facing entry, accommodation or deterrence, in an explicitly dynamic context. This basic choice involves sacrificing current profits to maintain market power over the medium to long run (the deterrence option) or earning high current returns at the cost of allowing entry (the accommodation option) and so suffering an erosion in market power over the medium to long run.

Gaskins [1971] was one of the first to characterize optimal pricing over time for an industry faced with a continous threat of entry. Gaskins specified entry as a flow rate of change of rival output $x(t)$ that depends on the price set by established firms, $p(t)$, and the rivals' long-run marginal cost, c_e:

$$dx(t)/dt = f(p(t), c_e) \tag{5}$$

Established firms choose a price path $p(t)$ to maximize total present value profits

$$\Pi_i = \int_{t=0}^{\infty} (p(t) - c_i)q(p(t),t)e^{-rt}dt \tag{6}$$

where c_i is the marginal production cost of the established firms, $q(p(t),t)$ is the difference between demand at price $p(t)$ and rival output x(t), and r is the incumbents' (assumed common) rate of time discount. With entry characterized by equation (5), the established firms' optimal price policy can be determined by the solution to a classical one control variable (p) and one state variable (x) optimal control problem. The optimal policy involves a tradeoff between the gains from monopoly pricing and the cost of entry induced by a high price. The more long sighted the incumbent and the slower is market growth, the more incumbents will be inclined to set prices low (relative to those which would be chosen by a myopic firm) in order to slow the rate at which entrants penetrate into the market. In practice, this means that price cuts will occur during periods when entrants are rapidly expanding (or could expand) their market share at the expense of incumbents. In a stationary market where the incumbent has no absolute cost advantages over entrants, price will approach competitive levels in the long run, and the market share of established firms will decline to zero.

This model tells a much richer story about market dynamics than the usual comparison of pre and post entry equilibria. Market power, in this view, is inherently transitory and the question of interest is how long it lasts. One line of empirical inquiry opened up by the model is concerned with the question of how fast (if at all) the shares of dominant firms decline in markets, and the evidence suggests that while many monopoly positions collapse shortly after their creation, those that do survive often survive for extremely long periods of time (e.g. Scherer [1980], pp, 239–42), Caves *et al.* [1984], Utton [1986], Geroski [1987], Mueller [1986], and others). Systematic evidence on the use of this type of entry regulation strategy paints a fairly mixed picture of its importance. Geroski [1988b] and Masson and Shaanan [1982] have applied econometric models to cross section data for the UK and US, detecting weak traces of evidence consistent with its use. The classic case study of this strategy in use is the decline of US steel which lost about 40 percentage points in market share in the 65 or so years following its creation (see Stigler [1965], but, for different views, see Parsons and Ray [1975] and Adams [1961]). Perhaps a clearer example was discussed by Shaw [1974] who looked at the response to entry in the retail petrol market in the UK. He observed the price cuts occurring during periods when the market shares of new entrants were rising most rapidly, a correlation which is consistent with the hypothesis. (Although it is also consistent with the alternate view that entrants provided post-entry price cuts.) One of the difficulties with trying to observe entry regulation in practice is that it is not always an optimal strategy for incumbents to follow, particularly when the market is growing rapidly. Brock [1975] applied the model to the US computer industry and discovered that it was unlikely to account for observed price and market share movements in what was an extremely rapidly growing market (see also Sengupta *et al.* [1983]).

Numerous variants of the basic dynamic limit pricing model exist. Kamien and Schwartz [1971] extended the Gaskins model to allow for stochastic entry. Flaherty [1980] introduced a model of rational entrant choice, but assumed that firms commit to output paths for all future time. This assumption is similar to the output commitment in the limit price model, and to the price path commitment in Gaskins [1971] and Kamien and Schwartz [1971], and is open to similar criticisms. Encaoua and Jacquemin [1980] extended the limit pricing model to include non-price strategic variables, and showed that price does not necessary approach the competitive level when other competitive weapons are available. Judd and Petersen [1986] introduced financing into the entry process and assumed that the rate of entry is governed by the need for firms to finance their expansions with internally-generated funds. The extent to which this is possible depends, of course, on the rate of profit, which the established firm(s) can control through its pricing decision. The connection between the pricing decision and the entrant's flow of funds to finance entry is a convenient way to make entry an endogenous feature of the model. Their results retain many of the features of Gaskins model, but differ in some predictions. For example, with slow growth, the optimal price drops to the fringe long-run marginal cost in finite time. If the market has a high initial growth rate and slows, the optimal price path may rise to a peak as the growth rate declines. While the market is growing it pays established firms to keep the price low and retard the growth of the fringe. When the growth rate slows, the established firms take their profits, and price gradually falls to a competitive level as the fringe continues to expand.

A difficulty with the Gaskins model and most of its successors is that the entry, equation (5), does not appear to result from optimizing decisions by potential entrants, but is specified exogenously in the model. The incumbent firm (or cartel) is presumed to act rationally, choosing a price policy to maximize present value profits, but firms are not symmetric in their degree of rationality.[26] Judd and Petersen [1986] introduce more rationality into the entry process, but the assumed constraint that entrants must finance their growth with internally generated funds is restrictive. Further, even if entry continues to the point where the incumbent firm makes up a very small share of the industry, it continues to act strategically while the behaviour of the new entrants is given exogenously. One can think of this as a basic ambiguity inherent in the nature of dominant firms as captured by the model. The way in which the asymmetry of roles is introduced in the model is totally exogenous, and the reasons why some firms act as leaders and some as followers is left unexplained. In fact, it could be more profitable to be a follower because the follower sells all of its desired quantity at the same price as the leader. The leader, on the contrary, is constrained by the reaction function of the follower. This argument is akin to the remark by Schelling [1960] that the role of leader is 'an unprofitable distinction evaded by the apparent follower and assumed per force by the apparent leader' (p. 23).

In the spirit of making these roles endogenous, Spence [1979] described a model in which firms are initially strategically similar, yet a form of leader-follower behaviour emerges. In Spence's model, firms are constrained in their maximum rates of growth. Either as a result of a head start or a larger maximum growth rate, one firm may attain a lead in the race for market share. At any point in the race, either firm may stop or continue to invest, thereby altering the future structure of the market. For example, suppose there are two firms, 1 and 2, and firm 1 is ahead. If both firms continue to invest, firm 2 will lose money. Through rapid growth, it is feasible for firm 1 to prevent the entry of firm 2, but firm 2 may threaten to remain in the market and, if its threat is taken seriously, firm 1 may choose to stop investing and accommodate its rival. The position in the race for market share gives each firm a

---

[26] The entry rate depends only on the current price, implying entry behaviour that is myopic. If nothing else, potential entrants should make use of the entry equation (5) to forecast future profitability. After all, if this is known to the incumbent firms(s), it should be common knowledge for the potential entrants as well. The one case in which this information has no value would be for potential entrants that have no investment at risk, e.g. if the investment required for entry is completely reversible.

menu of threats and counter threats that may influence the eventual structure of their market. Fudenberg and Tirole [1983] identify those threats which are credible in the Spence model, and show how they affect equilibrium industry structure.

The models developed by Spence [1979] and refined by Fudenberg and Tirole [1983] are examples of pre-emptive capacity expansion in which firms compete for the opportunity to serve all or a part of a market. Eaton and Lipsey [1979] study the incentives for market pre-emption in a model of location choice and Gilbert and Newbery [1982] examine pre-emptive activity in a competition for patents. In both of these situations, an established monopolist has an additional incentive to compete that is not available to a new entrant, namely the incentive to retain its monopoly power. Consider the following example. An established monopoly has profits equal to π^m. The entry occurs, either through locational expansion or the introduction of a new product by a competitor, the former monopolist will earn π_1^d and the new entrant will earn π_2^d. The entrant's incentive to become established in the industry is π_2^d. The monopolists incentive to prevent entry and retain a monopoly position is $\pi^m - \pi_1^d$. If entry has negative effect on industry profits (that is, if $\pi_1^d + \pi_2^d$ is less than π^m), the monopolists's incentive to prevent entry is larger than the incentive for a new firm to enter the market, and therefore the monopolist can spend more than an entrant can to build in anticipation of demand or to engage in R&D to patent a new technology.

The monopolists's extra incentive to protect its advantaged position would seem to provide a measure of security for an initial position of dominance, but there are other factors that work against this. This fact that a monopolist may depend on a cushion of profits from its base business can make new investment less attractive than it would be to a new competitor. This is the argument offered by Arrow [1962] and Reinganum [1983] for why a monopolist may be less, rather than more, inclined to invest in R&D. Gilbert [1986] examines the incentive for pre-emptive activity in a dynamic model of capacity expansion based on Gilbert and Harris [1984]. The incentive to invest in order to pre-empt the entry of a new firm depends, as in Dixit [1981], on whether an established monopolist would actually use any additional plant if entry were to occur. If excess capacity is not useful in the post-entry market, it is not a credible deterrent to entry. An established firm would be able to protect a monopoly position by investing before the earliest date at which entry would be profitable provided that entry precipitates aggressive competition, so that excess supply would be cleared by low prices.

In a growing market, successful pre-emption by an established firm would mean that the minimum efficient scale of entry eventually would be small relative to the size of the market. Small-scale entry would be unlikely to trigger a substantial competitive price response but without the price response, an established firm cannot make entry unprofitable by investing in extra capacity, because the extra capacity would not be used if entry were to occur. The conclusion of this exercise is that entry prevention by investment in anticipation of demand, as alleged in the case of U.S. v. Alcoa, is unlikely to be effective over the long term, although it can be of limited value in situations where potential rivals anticipate an aggressive price response to entry.

VI. EMPIRICAL MODELS OF ENTRY

A. Measuring the height of overall barriers

Having explored the major sources of entry barriers individually in Section III, it is time to assess the height of barriers overall, and thus the conditions of entry facing putative challengers. This is not quite as simple as 'summing up' the heights of the barriers created by product differentiation, scale economies, and absolute cost advantages because, as we have seen, these individual barriers derive much of their strength by interacting with other factors including, of course, the behaviour of incumbents. For example, modest scale economies can completely rule out entry in geographically segregated markets or in an already densely packed product space if established firms price aggressively in response to new competition. Introductory advertising campaigns can be impossibly expensive if consumers are reluctant to experiment with new suppliers. Finally, the combination of scale economies and the need for extensive pre- and post-sales servicing can force entrants to enter as a fully integrated concern, capital markets permitting. The point is that it is misleading to consider the effects of various types of barriers taken separately; it is the joint effect of all types of barriers taken together which is of interest.

Constructing an overall index is obviously an extremely difficult task given the problems we have already encountered in measuring particular types of barriers. Nevertheless, there appear to be two basic methods that can be followed. The first (Bain's method; see also Mann [1966]) relies heavily on the judgement and experience of the researcher to convert the ranking of industries by each individual source of barrier into a discontinuous overall scale, say 'high', and 'substantial', and 'moderate to low' (corresponding, Bain conjectured, to the ability to raise price persistently by 10%, 7% and not more than 4%, respectively, without attracting entry; p. 170). Thus, Bain considered automobiles (high scale economies, high product differentiation, high capital requirements, and low absolute cost barriers) in the same 'high' class as cigarettes (high product differentiation and capital requirements, low everything else) and fountain pens (only high product differentiation, if that). Steel (high absolute costs and capital requirements, low product differentiation and medium scale economies) ranked lower overall, and in the same 'substantial' barriers category is to be found shoes (medium scale economies and, perhaps, product differentiation, and low or zero everything else).

The second method of constructing estimates of the height of barriers was suggested by Orr [1974a]. The basic idea is to try to ascertain that level of profits which could be maintained indefinitely by incumbents without attracting entry. Suppose, for example, that for industries indexed by i, there is a 'limit rate of profit', π_i^*, which is sustainable permanently against entrants, and that if expected post-entry profits, π_i^e, exceed this rate, then entry, E_i, occurs. In particular, suppose that:

$$E_i = \Theta(\pi_i^e - \pi_i^*), \tag{7}$$

where π^e is expected post-entry profits and the entry response coefficient is Θ (and depends on the elasticity of industry demand, the expected response of incumbents and any short term costs of adjustment incurred by entrants[27]). π_i^*, the limit rate of profit, is unobserved, but one can suppose that it is determined by the individual types of barriers x_i^k where $k = 1$ is product differentiation barriers, and so on. Thus:

[27] Geroski and Murfin (1987a) and Geroski (1988c) derive (7) from an intertemporal optimization decision which entrants are assumed to use in selecting their optimal entry and post-entry market penetration strategies.

$$\pi_i^* = \alpha_0 + \alpha_1 x^1 + \ldots + \alpha_k x^k, \tag{8}$$

where there are k types of barriers (some of the x^k may interact). Inserting (8) into (7), one can estimate the unknown parameters Θ, α_o, ..., α_k using the observed variables E_i, x^1, ... x^k and a proxy for π_i^e. Substituting into (7) enables one to estimate the parameters α_o, ..., α_k, and so generate an estimate of π_i^*. This estimate of π_i^* is obviously *an* index of the height of barriers overall (or actually normalizes it so that positive values signal high barriers), since, by definition, limit profits are those sustainable forever without encouraging entry. As an index of the overall height of entry barriers, π_i^* has the following advantages: it is continuous; the weight of each individual barrier is empirically determined, presumably in accordance with its contribution to deterring entry; it is easy to calculate standard errors of the estimates; and, finally, the natural uncertainty that one has about whether (7) and (8) form the correct model can be reduced by considering how robust the calculations are to various changes in model specification.

There now have been several studies of entry which have followed the same basic methodology as Orr.[28] While many of these have developed and explored the model in interesting ways, what is important for our purposes here is the general tenor of the results on the sizes of π_i^*, on its determinants and on Θ. The measure of agreement across these studies is fairly high. π_i^* generally rises in advertising intensity, capital intensity, minimum efficient scale, diversification, multiplant economies and economies of scope. Increases in industry growth and market size lower π_i^*, while industry concentration and R&D intensity have mixed effects. Both Geroski [1988c] and Geroski [1988b] have computed the levels of price-cost margins sustainable forever against entry (i.e. π_i^*) and, in the U.K., discovered them to be quite high (about 17%), and fairly similar for both domestic entrants and foreign based entrants. Gorecki [1975, 1976] has made comparisons between domestic and foreign and new and diversifying entrants, and has found that they face different types of barriers and react with somewhat different speeds. Estimates of Θ have also been

[28] See Duetsch, [1975, 1984], and Gorecki, [1975, 1976], Gorecki and Baldwin, [1983, 1986]), Hamilton [1985], Harris, [1973, 1976], Highfield and Smiley, [1987], Khemani and Shapiro, [1985, 1986], MacDonald, [1986], Masson and Shaanan, [1986], Schwalbach, [1987], Shapiro, [1983], Yip, [1982], Hirshey, [1981], and others.

rather mixed, with a clutch of studies producing results similar to Orr (i.e. $\Theta \simeq 0$). Even when Θ has been estimated as significantly different from zero, it appears to be rather small, and simulations suggest that these estimated values of Θ imply an extremely weak and sluggish feedback between entry and profits [e.g. Geroski and Masson, 1987]. In fact, estimates of Θ turn out to be rather sensitive to the details of how π_i^e is proxied. Most studies use lagged profits as a proxy, but those that use rational expectations or extrapolative predictors generate higher, more significant values of Θ. For example, Geroski [1988c] and Geroski [1988] have discovered Θ to be virtually identical between domestic and foreign entrants into the UK, to be relatively constant across industries, and to be much larger and more significant when a rational expectations proxy of π_i^e is used rather than when lagged profits or an extrapolative predictor is used.

B. The interaction between entry and profits

High entry barriers are a pre-condition for above-normal profits in an industry. Without significant barriers, entry (if only of the 'hit-and-run' variety) can be relied upon to eliminate excess profits. This suggests that the presence of entry barriers can be detected by the persistence of high profits, and raises the broader question of how fast entry reacts to profits and how fast the effects of entry make themselves felt in profits. To treat this problem fully, one needs to chart both the effect of profits in attracting entry, and the effect entrants have on subsequent profitability, and this requires going beyond the simple entry equation (1).

Two rather different first steps in this direction were take by Duetsch [1975] and Stonebraker [1976]. In Duetsch's model, the percentage change in the number of firms is explained by profitability which, in turn, is dependent on a number of factors, including conventional measures of entry barriers, concentration, diversification and growth. Comparing the 1958–63 period in the U.S. with 1963–67, Duetsch found that large increases in diversification over the period reduced entry; advertising, growth and concentration had familiar positive and significant effects on profits, and negative effects on entry. Stonebraker's model is a little more elaborate. The profits of large firms, π^L, are taken to increase in 'entry risk', R, which reflects the effects of traditional barriers of measuring the likelihood of failure of entrants. Entry risk is measured operationally by examining the actual profit-loss record of small firms, and is explained by barriers X_j. Hence:

$$\pi_i^L = y_0 + y_1 \mathrm{R} + \delta_2 Z_1 + \delta_3 Z_2 \quad (9)$$

$$R_i = \delta_0 + \delta_1 X_1 + \ldots + \delta_4 X_4, \quad (10)$$

where Z_1 is the percentage of loss making firms in the industry, Z_2 is growth, and $X_1, \ldots, X_4$ are four barriers that reflect advertising, research, economies of scale, and the absolute size of plants. α_1, α_2 and α_3 were all found to be positive and significant, as were the coefficients on advertising and research barriers for a sample of 33 U.S. industries. The entry mechanism is also implicit in this model, high π^L being presumably caused by low entry, the latter being determined by R, entry risk, and, in turn determining it.

Both these models recognize that there are important interactions between entry and profitability to keep track of in tracing the consequences of entry barriers, although in both cases the dynamic feedback between the two is implicit and unexplored. The model of Masson and Shaanan [1982] extends the notion of using profits as a signal by explicitly recognizing that it may reflect systematic distortions by firms anxious to hide excess profits from entrants, or discourage entry through limit pricing. In their model, entry is conceived to be determined in a manner similar to that of Orr:

$$E(t)_i = \Theta(\pi_i(t-1) - \pi_i^*) \quad (11)$$

where the lags are imposed on the data (e.g. $t-1$ is average 1950–57 values, t is 1958–63) and E(t) is entrant market shares. As before, limit profits, π_i^*, are determined by conventional barriers (advertising, absolute cost advantages, scale economies) and industry growth, collectively X_j,

$$\pi_i^* = \sum \alpha_j X_j. \quad (12)$$

(11) and (12) together describe the 'entry reaction function'; i.e. entrants' behaviour. Incumbents, in response to this, choose strategies yielding some target level of profits. If all incumbents operated collusively, this target, π^0, would be given by:

$$\pi_i^0 = \sum_{k=1}^{K} \beta_k W_k, \tag{13}$$

where the factors W_k include advertising, growth, minimum efficient scale, and absolute cost requirements. If industry members do not act collusively, then only some fraction of target profits are assumed to be achieved. The relation between actual profits, π, and the target, π^0, depends on the extent of collusion, and Masson and Shaanan express this as,

$$\pi_i(t) = \pi_i^0 + \delta(\text{CON}(t) - 100), \tag{14}$$

where CON(t) is the concentration ratio. In this system, entry barriers play two roles, affecting entry rates via (11)–(12) on the one hand, and limit profit behaviour and thus profits directly via (12)–(13) on the other. Profits affect entry via (11), and entry subsequently feeds back profits in (14) to the extent that CON is reduced. The crucial parameters which capture this feedback are δ and Θ. Masson and Shaanan estimated the E(t) equation derived from (11)–(12) jointly with the $\pi(t-1)$ equation from (13)–(14), deriving estimates of $\Theta \approx .5$ and $\delta \approx .5$. Their estimates of the α_j suggest the existence of important scale but not growth effects on entry and, by comparing estimated values of π^* and π^0, concluded that entry was 'regulated' by incumbents and not foreclosed.[29] Their estimate of $\pi_i^* = 8.42\%$ and $\pi_i^0 = 13.84\%$ on average.

The estimates of Θ, δ and the α_j reported by Masson and Shaanan are fairly typical of the literature, and it is worth asking what they imply about the short run dynamics of entry. To describe a full feedback loop between profits and entry, one needs to establish a link between $E(t)$ in (11) and CON in (14). Geroski and Masson [1987] added

$$\text{CON}(t) = \Omega E(t), \tag{15}$$

$\Omega < 0$, to (11)–(14), and assumed that $\Omega = -1$ (i.e. that entrants take market share away from only the leading firms in the market).[30] Using

[29] Masson and Shaanan [1983] have used this model to calculate monopoly dead weight loss, finding that *actual* losses were substantially less than *potential* losses. As a check on the Masson and Shaanan [1982] numbers, note the similar estimates of Θ and several other parameters by Harris, [1976b], who used basically the same data.

[30] For some work on the indirect effects of entry barriers on market structure, see Mueller and Hamm [1974], Wright [1978], Mueller and Rogers [1980], Caves and Porter

(15), (14) can be transformed into a relationship between $\pi(t)$ and all previous entry into the industry. (11) links $E(t)$ to $\pi(t-1)$ in every t, and using that in (14) produces a difference equation in $\pi(t)$. The long run equilibrium implicit in this equation is π^*, and the equation describes the movements to π^* from any arbitrary starting point caused by entry. As it happens, the Masson and Shaanan estimates imply that this difference equation is roughly of order 1, and the coefficient on $\pi(t-1)$ implies extremely slow convergence of $\pi(t)$ towards π^* for any initial disturbance. In particular, starting the system off at $\pi(0) = 13.84\%$, it takes roughly seventy years to move $\pi(t)$ halfway towards $\pi^* = 8.42\%$. Further, since most entrants take market share away from small firms and not market leaders (implying that Ω is close to zero), these estimates, if anything, overstate the speed with which the competitive process works.

It is, of course, difficult to believe that the competitive process is as slow as these numbers imply, and there are at least two problems which are likely to have led to a possibly major understatement of the effects of entry. First, the Masson and Shaanan data may understate the true volume of actual entry, not least because it does not take account of foreign based entry. Systematic understatement of $E(t)$ will bias down estimates of Θ, understate changes in CON(t) and thus understate induced changes in $\pi(t)$. Second, using observed entry flows to measure the competitive effect of the challenge that entrants present to incumbents may understate the size of that challenge, not least because entry need not actually occur to have an impact on market performance. As we have seen, there is a range of pre-entry strategic investments that will pre-empt entrants, and many of these are likely to reduce profits to some degree. Limit pricing, for example, involves a sacrifice in current profits for a higher future flow (relative to what would occur if entry were not blocked), and this will appear in the data as a movement in $\pi(t)$ towards π^* unaccompanied by entry.

There are several ways to handle this type of problem. The simplest is to treat $E(t)$ as an unobservable, latent variable rather than using what might be a systematically biased measure of it. If $E(t)$ cannot be

---

[1980], Jenny and Weber [1978], Kamerschen [1968], McGuckin [1972], Dorwood [1977], Geroski *et al.* [1987], and others; and, for work on market share stability, see Gort [1962], Caves and Porter [1978], and Meisel [1981]. Curry and George [1983], is a good survey of much of this material.

observed, then (11) and (15) cannot be estimated (i.e. one cannot obtain estimates of Θ and Ω). However, since entry in period t is caused by $\pi(t-1)$ and affects $\pi(t)$, $\pi(t+1)$, ..., then the workings of the competitive feedback mechanism can be observed simply by looking at a times series on $\pi_i(t)$. Using, for example, a model like

$$\pi_i(t) = \alpha_i + \beta\pi_i(t-1), \tag{16}$$

yields an estimate of π_i^* given by the long run solution to (16), namely $\alpha_i/(1-\beta)$, and an estimate of the speed of the process, $\Theta\Omega\delta$, given by β. The Geroski–Masson simulations used the Masson–Shaanan estimates of Θ, Ω and δ to estimate β, but, if these are indeed biased, a simpler procedure would be to estimate (16) directly. There is now a fairly large literature which has done just exactly this, estimating (16) for leading firms as well as at the industry level.[31] The estimates of β obtained in these studies is considerably lower than that implicit in the Masson–Shaanan estimates, suggesting that the convergence of $\pi_i(t)$ to π_i^* is far more rapid than our previous estimate suggested. This is, of course, exactly what one might suspect if $E(t)$ were underestimated because imports were neglected, and if measures of observed entry flows understated the full competitive threat posed by entrants, actual and potential.

This particular solution to the problem of measuring the size of the entry challenge that incumbents face is rather extreme, and has the considerable drawback of totally neglecting the information that is contained in actual entry flows. The basic message of the work that we have discussed thus far is that there may be two types of dynamic movements in $\pi_i(t)$ associated with entry. The first arises as actual entry occurs, leading to an increase in the degree of competition and so to a bidding away of excess profits. The second movement in $\pi_i(t)$ arises in anticipation of entry as incumbents attempt to block entry, and will not, by definition, be associated with actual entry flows. The type of empirical model that this calls for is a two equation model of entry and profits in which the profits equation is general enough to trace both types of effects associated with entry. Geroski [1988b] has derived such

[31] This work has been done at industry and at firm specific levels for several countries; see, for example, Mueller [1977, 1986], Connolly and Schwartz [1985], Cubbin and Geroski [1987], Geroski and Jacquemin [1988], Levy [1987], Ogadiri and Yamawaki [1986] and others. Mueller [1986], in particular, has focused on extracting estimates of π^*_i from (7), and finds important correlations with market share and advertising.

a model from the Gaskins model discussed above, effectively combining an entry equation like (11) with a profits equation.

$$\pi_i(t) = \alpha_i + \beta\pi_i(t-1) - \lambda \sum_{\tau=0}^{\infty} E(t-\tau). \tag{17}$$

β, as before, reflects movements in $\pi_i(t)$ associated with regulation of entry by incumbents while λ reflects the effects that actual entry has on profits. Applied to 85 UK industries for 1974–79, the estimates suggested rather rapid convergence of $\pi_i(t)$ to long run profits, π_i^*, with perhaps as much as half the effect being associated with actual entry flows. Like Masson and Shaanan, these estimates imply that at least some strategic pre-emption of entry occurs, but the very high level of the estimated barriers to entry suggest that the potential impact of entry is rather modest. Entry is a quick but probably quite incomplete method of reducing profits in most markets. Geroski also observed that both λ and β varied systematically across industries, and that the dynamics of the entry process were slower in more advertising intensive, highly concentrated markets.

The role of advertising seems of some importance in many markets subject to entry, and it is unlikely to be exogenous to the entry competition process. An obvious extension of the models that we have examined thus far has been explored by Geroski and Murfin [1987a], who developed a three equation model involving entry and subsequent market expansion, advertising and profits applied to a 25 year panel for the UK Car Industry. They use the advertising and profits equations to generate rational expectations proxies of post-entry profits and advertising, seeking a statistically acceptable dynamic specification of their model in order to compute short and long run effects of various factors on entry. What emerges clearly from their regression and simulation results is the important effect that advertising has on the market share penetration of entrants and, despite a 30% fall during the sample period, the weak effect of declines on entry penetration. In this sector at least, entry sparked off a major advertising war post-entry. Prices appeared to have been relatively unaffected by entry, and the explosion in advertising not only helped to maintain industry price-cost margins at high levels despite entry, but actually led to a small post-entry rise.

Thus, the general tenor of much of the empirical work that has been done on the effect of entry on profits is that the impact of entry is fairly modest. These results suggest that entry barriers are high in many industries (or that markets are in equilibrium and there isn't much entry of consequence), and, while the return of profits to long run levels may be fairly rapid, these long run levels seem to be rather high. Incumbents, it seems, can maintain fairly reasonable mark ups on costs more or less indefinitely in the face of entry. There are, however, at least three reasons to treat these conclusions with caution. First, there is no doubt that accounting data on profits are rather noisy indicators of the economic profits, and one cannot hope to draw really firm conclusions without a more detailed examination of costs and demand.[32] This is compounded by the problem of arbitrary cost allocations in multiproduct firms. Second, since the threat of entry may lead incumbents to remove X-inefficiency and slack, then profits after entry may be relatively constant even when entry has a dramatic effect on price. To the extent that this is the case, then the impact of entry on profits is likely to understate its effect on prices. Third, it is more than possible that the studies discussed above have exaggerated the height of entry barriers. In Geroski [1988b], for example, only six years of data was examined and, if the post-entry penetration of most entrants is sufficiently slow, then it might take ten to fifteen years before the full competitive effect of entry materializes. What looks like high long run margins from the perspective of six years may, in fact, look far more modest from the point of view of ten to fifteen years. The bottom line, then, is that the effects of entry are slow to materialize, and may even be modest in the truly long run.

C. Other models of entry

Simple entry models based on (11), and even multi-equation models built around a system like (11)–(15), seem to be a natural first solution to the problem of inferring something about entry barriers from entry flows and the short run impact of entry on market performance. Entry is generally imagined to respond to very simple and straightforward

---

[32] Although it is possible to construct examples in which accounting and economic profits diverge spectacularly (e.g. Fisher and McGowan [1983]), in practice the two are highly correlated and systematic divergence appears to depend mainly on firm size (e.g. Salamon [1985]). Furthermore, persistently high (low) accounting returns imply persistently high (low) economic returns (e.g. Kay and Mayer [1986]).

signals like current or lagged profits, and to be blocked in a quantity proportional to a linear combination of entry barriers. One extracts from such a model weights to convert individual entry barriers into an overall index of the condition of entry, an estimate of the size and speed of the response by entrants to profits signals, and an estimate of their effects on profits. However, this methodology by no means exhausts the range of interesting empirical questions that one can ask about entry; nor is it the only methodology that one can use to infer something about entry barriers from entry rates. It is, therefore, worth briefly exploring a number of alternative models.

One major problem with the use of simple profit signals to model entry flows is that rational entrants will not be attracted by pre- so much as post-entry profitability. The desire to model this post-entry situation carefully is a major concern in Kessides [1986]. His starting point is to assume that the number of new firms, N_e, that are recorded in the data is such as to set expected post-entry profits to zero. To model the latter, suppose that the good in question is homogeneous, that pre-entry price is p_o, and that the efficient scale of entry is x. Then, the arrival of N_e entrants results in a post-entry price, p_e, of approximately

$$p_e \approx p_o[1 - N_e s]/\eta, \tag{18}$$

where η is the absolute value of the price elasticity of demand and $s \equiv x/q_o$, the ratio of the efficient scale of entry to pre-entry output. Clearly, the change in price due to entry, $\Delta p \equiv p_e - p_o$, is

$$\Delta p = -p_o[N_e s]/\eta. \tag{19}$$

Letting exogenous market growth occur at a rate g and letting the expansion rate of incumbents be r, then (19) can be generalized to

$$\Delta p = -p_o[N_e s - (g - r)]/\eta(1 + g). \tag{20}$$

Equation (20) tells a simple straightforward story. If the market grows fast enough or if incumbents cut back their output post-entry, then post-entry prices could actually exceed pre-entry prices. In all cases, a more elastic demand leads to a smaller price change, as does a smaller efficient scale of entry and a smaller number of entrants. Advertising enters the model hold as a sunk cost of entry and as a possible determinant of whether to respond to entry or not. Kessides applied this model to data on the net number of new firms in 266 four digit U.S.

industries, 1972–1977. His results suggest that advertising gives rise to a sunk cost barrier to entry, and that advertising is more important than physical capital in creating sunk costs which deter entry. Further, he concluded that entrants perceive a greater likelihood of success in highly advertising intensive markets, that incumbents are more likely to respond to entry the higher are pre-entry profits, π_o, and the higher is market concentration, and, finally, that $g \approx r$ on average.

One of the useful features of the Kessides model is that it makes plain the fact that the expected returns to entry depend upon how many entrants simultaneously enter, and a model which explores this interaction between entrants more thoroughly has been discussed by Bresnahan and Reiss [1986]. They consider a set of markets in which only one of three market structures can occur post-entry: no entry, monopoly, or duopoly. Letting monopoly profits be π^M and duopoly profits be $\pi^D < \pi^M$, then the probabilities of observing any of these outcomes is

$$\begin{aligned} Pr\{N=0\} &= Pr\{\pi^M < 0\}, \\ Pr\{N=2\} &= Pr\{\pi^D > 0), \\ Pr\{N=1\} &= 1 - Pr\{N=0\} - Pr\{N=2\}. \end{aligned} \tag{21}$$

The events $N=0$, 1, 2 are observed, but π^M and π^D are not and must be inferred from the data using (21). To give some structure to the problem, Bresnahan and Reiss suppose that price, p, depends on per capita demand, q, but is homogeneous of degree zero in market size, z. Then, profits, V, are given by

$$\mathrm{V} = [p(q) - c]qz - f, \tag{22}$$

where f is fixed costs and c is marginal costs. The important point about the structure of (22) is that equilibrium quantities and prices are independent of z. Thus, at any equilibrium price p^* and quantities q* (e.g. the monopoly or duopoly equilibrium), profits are

$$V = mz - f, \tag{23}$$

where $m \equiv q^*[p(q^*) - c]$. It follows that post-entry returns are linear in z. Substituting (23) into (21) and doing the appropriate profit regressions, the difference between monopoly and duopoly outcomes can be observed by differences in the co-efficient on z. Bresnahan and Reiss applied the model to data on retail automobile dealerships in small, well defined, local markets in the U.S. in 1982, and observed that an entrant into a monopoly market would earn about 66% of the variable profits of the original monopolist; i.e. that entry does not substantially affect price-cost margins. They also observed that the response by entrants to market growth was very slow with lags of ten years or more observed in the data.

The basic source of interaction between entrants arises from the fact that entry by one entrant reduces the potential post-entry gains available to other entrants. If, for example, one type of entrant is faster to enter than a second type, faces lower barriers and has a bigger impact on profits, then one expects to observe it crowding out other types. For example, suppose that entrants of type a behave according to

$$E_a(t) = \Theta_a\{\pi(t-1) - \pi_a^*\} \tag{24}$$

and entrants of type b according to

$$E_b(t) = \Theta_b\{\pi(t-1) - \pi_b^*\}. \tag{25}$$

Both entrants have an effect on profits, which we model as

$$\pi(t) = \alpha + \beta\pi(t-1) + \lambda_a \sum_{\tau=0}^{\infty} E_a(t-\tau) + \lambda_b \sum_{\tau=0}^{\infty} E_b(t-\tau) \tag{26}$$

If $\Theta_a > \Theta_b$ and $\lambda_a > \lambda_b$, then entrants of type *a* will tend to arrive faster than *b*, and, because a's impact on $\pi(t)$ is much larger than *b*'s, any given volume of $E_a(t)$ leaves room for less $E_b(t)$ than an equivalent volume of $E_b(t)$ leaves for $E_a(t)$. In these circumstances, entry by *a* will tend to crowd out entry by *b*. Geroski [1988a] applied this type of model to foreign and domestic entry in the U.K., 1974–1979, and observed no noticeable tendency for either type of entrant to crowd out the other. Indeed, the data suggested that the two types of entrants interacted very little, implying that they were likely to be entering rather different market segments and not, in general, competing directly with each other.

None of the models discussed this far examine the entry decision explicitly in terms of the type of entry strategy that entrants elect to use. One of the more interesting of these strategies is advertising. It seems clear that the judicious use of advertising can facilitate entry, and one of the questions that one wishes to ask using a model of entry and advertising is how advertising might affect consumer behaviour in a way that facilitates entry. Geroski and Murfin [1987b] have explored a particular model along these lines, applying it to entry into the U.K. car market. The basic postulates they adopted were three: that prices vary less than the quality of different brands, that a single purchase does not give full information to consumers about the quality, v_i, of the brand (i) chosen, and that the quality of each brand varies over time and so consumers act as if they have a short memory. The implications of these are quite powerful. Buyer behaviour is stochastic in this model, and, since the consumer is not exactly sure of v_i, nor of any of the v_j, $j \neq i$, satisfaction does not guarantee a repeat purchase. Suppose that if s/he is satisfied, s/he repeats the purchase in the next period, t, with probability $(1 - 1/v_i)$. In the event of dissatisfaction, the consumer must choose an alternative brand, and Geroski and Murfin suppose that s/he does so on the basis of the volume of advertising of the different brands. They assume that the probability of selecting brand j at t is proportional to brand j's advertising share, $a_j(t)$. Thus, the probability of a switch from brand i to brand j by some consumer is

$$p_{ij}(t) = (1 - 1/v_i)\delta_{ij} + a_j(t)/v_i, \tag{27}$$

where $\delta_{ij} = 1$ for $i = j$, and is zero otherwise. At a long run equilibrium at which all firms maintain stable levels of advertising, the probability of any one consumer selecting brand i is approximately $a_i\tilde{N}_i$, where $\tilde{N}_i$ depends on the full vector of v_i's. With a large number of independent buyers, this probability is also the market share of brand i. Thus, for an entrant brand i into a market with total revenue R and price-cost margin π expected post-entry profits are

$$V_i = \tilde{N}_i a_i \pi R - f, \tag{28}$$

where f is fixed costs. The entrant's decision rule is then to enter if it thinks that it can capture an advertising share greater than $f/\tilde{N}_i R\pi$ post-entry, and to stay out otherwise. Geroski and Murfin found (28) to be surprisingly accurate in its predictions about when entry occurred, and the order in which entrants entered the three segments of the market that they considered. Advertising share proved to be a powerful predictor of entry, and the elasticity of the probability of entry with respect to advertising proved to be nearly 50% higher for later than for earlier entrants. While advertising facilitated entry in the sense that successful entry followed the achievement of a large enough advertising share, Geroski and Murfin also observed that the probability of entry fell as industry wide advertising totals rose; i.e.

that the incidence of entry fell as the costs of achieving the critical advertising share rose.

Although virtually all of the work thus far discussed presumes that entry is driven by excess profits, this is a presumption which ought to be questioned for at least two reasons. First, while entrants are bound to be interested in the present discounted value of profits over their expected life in the industry, it is not clear that current profits are a terribly good signal of that quantity. What may be much more important than current period market conditions is the likely evolution of the market over time. One plausible indicator of this future is, of course, industry growth; another is current changes in technology. Second, when incumbent firms experience costs to adjusting their existing capital stock, then high industry growth may enable entrants to squeeze into the market, even when prices are close to marginal costs.

Hause and Du Reitz, [1984], have explored this latter possibility in a model applied to Swedish data. They discovered the expected positive correlations between entry and growth, noting also that high minimum efficient scale and the presence of explicit cartel agreements were associated with lower entry rates. Whether it is reasonable to follow Hause and Du Reitz in assuming that growth is exogenous to entry is problematic, particularly for innovative entrants or for those entrants who spark off market increasing non-price post-entry wars. Finally, Hause and Du Reitz noted strong heteroscedasticity in their results, i.e. that the probability of entry given the five independent variables used varied across sectors. This means either the omission of important variables in their model, or that entry is not normally distributed (the correct distribution appears to be one in which the variance of the distribution rises in its mean, a natural type of distribution for a non-negative variable). Gort and Konakayama, [1982], explored a model in which entry is driven, *inter alia*, by technological change. Evidence from a sample of seven industries suggested that major innovations and the incidence of patenting both seem to be positively associated with entry, at least in early phases of the industry life cycle.

VII. CONCLUDING REMARKS

This long and, at times, somewhat detailed survey of the literature on entry has, in the main, sought to identify the major features of that literature. It is, however, impossible to conclude such a survey without making a number of broader observations about the literature and its implications for policy.

At the theoretical level, we have seen that barriers to the movement of capital may be defined in different ways with different consequences for both the measurement of barriers to entry and exit and for the implications of measured barriers on economic welfare. Concerning conditions of entry, the structuralist view proposes a taxonomy based on scale economies, cost advantages, and product differentiation, that reflects the combined incidence of technological features of markets and the behaviour of the firms in these markets. For example, the extent to which economies of scale represent a barrier to entry depends on whether the technology permits established firms to deny equally efficient new competitors an equal market share. This is implicit in Bain's characterization of the 'percentage effect' of entry at large scale and it is the cornerstone of the classical BSM model of limit pricing. Stigler's objection to the identification of economies of scale as an entry barrier rests squarely on the relevance of demand constraints to the profitability of entry. We have argued that if economies of scale permit established firms to limit the market available to new entrants, then they are a source of entry barriers. We showed how this situation may come about when production involves substantial sunk costs. In this way, strategy and structure may interact to create barriers and to sustain profitable operations by established firms.

A central feature of the literature is the view that much of the variations in the outcome of market competition, be it in price or in production, springs from variations in initial conditions which in turn arise from strategic choices made in antecedent games such as R&D or location choices (Geroski and Jacquemin [1984]). Such a precommitment to a strategic position narrows the range of replies open to rivals and creates a differential movement advantage. This does not imply that dominance ought to be equated with first mover advantages, since in some games movements by the first firm expand the choice set of the second mover and create follower advantages. Similarly, a price leader cannot necessarily be identified as a dominant firm if this leader enjoys no specific advantage. What this suggests is that a satisfactory explanation of observed asymmetries depends on the history of entry into an industry. The emergence of successful entrants relies on successive processes including the generation of players from agents having invested in information, the generation of trials from players and the generation of successful outcomes from trials, leading to dominant positions that affect outcomes and can be sustained over time.

The general impression suggested by our review of empirical work is the difficulty of measuring adequately the various types of barriers, their overall height, and estimating their impact on market performance. The results we have, however, suggest that while markets often appear to be relatively competitive, that degree of competitiveness is far from perfect and many firms enjoy some degree of market power for what are sometimes appreciable lengths of time. The potential impact of entry seems to be modest. Entrants usually do not take much market share from industries leaders but instead tend to take a market share from small incumbents Post-entry survival is not easy. Two specific aspects of these results can be underlined. First, there is some discrepancy between, on the one hand, the long list of possible structural factors and strategic behaviour that is able in principle, to deter entry, and, on the other hand, the empirical observatories suggesting that there is only a limited exploitation of these possibilities by incumbent firms. Although some strategic actions appear to be relatively widely used, (such as spatial pre-emption, brand proliferation and advertising giving rise to sunk costs), there seems to be some reason to believe that the response to entry is rather selective. Second, a growing number of studies show that superior profits persist over time, as well as interfirm profitability differences. The findings that profit rates of large firms do not converge over time to a common mean are clearly incompatible with the theory of perfectly contestable markets, but are consistent with various dynamic models of dominant firm behaviour.

The welfare implications of these results are complex. It is clear that prices may be held substantially above competitive levels for long periods of time, leading to important welfare losses. However, in several cases, trade-offs can appear (see also Jacquemin and Slade [1989]). When scale and scope economies exist over a broad range of outputs or when there is a variety of products, few firms may be preferred to many, so that a policy designed to increase the number of firms would result in reduced social welfare. With dynamic effects such as learning and technical change, the issues are even more complex, and there can exist a trade-off between cost reduction or innovation on the one hand and intensity of competition and entry on the other.[33] In spite of these uncertainties, both the theoretical arguments and the empirical indications provided by our survey suggest the very limited relevance of the model of perfectly contestable markets for explaining the real world. This theory depends on the heroic assumptions of markets free of any barrier to capital mobility and of prices moving slowly relative to capital. On the other hand industry studies (e.g. Mueller [1986]) reveal several relatively robust results, including large profits variability in the short run and persistent dispersion of profitability among large firms that are not compatible with the implications of the model.

On the basis of our survey, some tentative suggestions for *industry policy* can finally be made. Clearly, ease of entry in a market must receive an important weight when evaluating the possible anti-competitive effects of a given conduct. However, ease of entry is not a sufficient condition for allowing conduct substantially restricting competition among existing firms: given the limits of contestability theory and the often long time taken for entering a market, potential competition is not a perfect substitute for competition among incumbent firms. The possibility that some barriers to entry may raise efficiency must be recognized and dealt with on a case by case basis. In our second-best world, adopting fine-tuned 'optimal' rules to identify precisely the efficiency consequences of business conduct would be presumptuous, but a system of *per se* rules, although, easier to administer, runs the risk of ignoring subtle differences in the interaction between strategy and structure and may obscure the large variance in their consequences for economic performance in different markets.

REFERENCES

Adams, W. and J. Brock (1982), 'Integrated Monopoly and Market Power: System Selling Compatibility Standards, and Market Control', *Quarterly Review of Economics and Business*, **22**, 29–42.

Adams, W. (1961) 'The Steel Industry', in Adams W. (ed) *The Structure of American Industry*, Macmillan, New York.

---

[33] In the context of the growing internationalization of many markets which increase their size, it can be expected that such trade-offs will be less frequent than in closed economies, but this cannot be a general answer to the problem, given that the number of entrants is also growing.

Aghion, P. and P. Bolton (1986), 'Entry Prevention through Contracts with Customers', MIT working paper.

Arrow, K. (1962), 'Economic Welfare and the Allocation of Resources for Inventions', in Nelson, R. (ed). *The Rate and Direction of Invention Activity*, Princeton University Press.

Ayanian, R. (1975), 'Advertising and the Rate of Return', *Journal of Law and Economics*, **18**, 479-506.

Bailey, E. (1986), 'Price and Productivity Change Following Deregulation: The US Experience', *Economic Journal*, **96**, 1-17.

Bailey, E. and J. Panzar (1981), 'The Contestability of Airline Markets during the Transition to Deregulation', *Law and Contemporary Problems*, **44**, 125-145.

Bailey, E., D. Graham and D. Kaplan (1984), *Deregulating the Airlines: An Economic Analysis*, MIT Press, Cambridge, Mass.

Bain, J. (1956), *Barriers to New Competition*, Harvard University Press, Cambridge, Mass.

Baumol, W., J. Panzar and R. Willig (1982), *Contestable Markets and the Theory of Industry Structure*, Harcourt Brace Jovanovich, San Diego.

Baumol, W., J. Panzar and R. Willig (1986), 'On the Theory of Perfectly Contestable Markets', in Stiglitz, J. and F. Mathewson (Eds.), *New Developments in the Analysis of Market Structure*, MIT Press, Cambridge, Mass.

Baumol, W. and R. Willig (1981), 'Fixed Cost, Sunk Cost, Entry Barriers and the Sustainability of Monopoly', *Quarterly Journal of Economics*, **95**, 405-431.

Baumol, W. and R. Willig (1986), 'Contestability: Developments Since the Book', C. V. Starr Center for Applied Economics, New York University.

Benham, L. (1972), 'The Effect of Advertising on the Price of Eyeglasses', *Journal of Law and Economics*, **15**, 337-352.

Bernheim, D. (1984), 'Strategic Deterrence of Sequential Entry into an Industry', *Rand Journal of Economics*, **15**, 1-12.

Brock, W. and J. Scheinkman (1983), 'Free Entry and the Sustainability of Natural Monopoly', in Evans, D. (ed) *Breaking up Bell: Essays on Industrial Organization and Regulation*, North Holland, Amsterdam.

Chamberlin, E. (1933), 'The Theory of Monopolistic Competition', *Harvard University Press*, Cambridge, Mass.

Bevan, A. (1974), 'The UK Potato Crisp Industry 1960-72: A Study of New Entry Competition', *Journal of Industrial Economics*, **22**, 281-297.

Biggadike, E. (1976), *Corporate Diversification: Entry, Strategy and Performance*, Division of Research, Graduate School of Business Administration, Harvard University, Boston.

Blackstone, E. (1972), 'Limit Pricing and Entry in the Copying Machine Industry', *Quarterly Review of Economics and Business*, **12**, 57-65.

Block, H. (1974), 'Advertising and Profitability: A Reappraisal', *Journal of Political Economy*, **82**, 267-86.

Bond, R. and D. Lean (1977), 'Sales, Promotion and Product Differentiation in Two Prescription Drugs Markets', mimeo, FTC.

Boyer, K. (1974), 'Informative and Goodwill Advertising', *Review of Economics and Statistics*, **56**, 541-48.

Bresnahan, T. (1985), 'Post-Entry Competition in the Plain Paper Copier Market, *American Economic Review Papers and Proceedings*, **75**, 15-19.

Bresnahan, T. and R. Reiss (1986), 'Entry in Monopoly Markets', mimeo, Stanford University.

Brock, G. (1975), *The US Computer Industry: A Study of Market Power*, Ballinger, Cambridge, Mass.

Brown, R. (1978), 'Estimating Advantages to Large Scale Advertising', *Review of Economics and Statistics*, **60**, 428–37.

Bulow, J., Geanakopolis J. and Klemperer, P. (1985), Multimarket Oligopoly: Strategic substitutes and Complements, *Journal of Political Economy*, **93**, 488–511.

Butters, G. (1976), 'A survey of Advertising and Market Structure', *American Economic Review*, **66**, 392–7.

Call G. and T. Keeler (1985), 'Airline Deregulation, Fares and Market Behaviour. Some Empirical Evidence', in A. Daugherty (ed.), *Analytical Studies in Transport Economics*, Cambridge University Press, Cambridge.

Caves, R., J. Khalilzaden-Shiraz and M. Porter (1975), 'Scale Economies in Statistical Analyses of Market Power', *Review of Economics and Statistics*, **57**, 133–40.

Caves, R., M. Fortunato and P. Ghemawat (1984), 'The Decline of Dominant Firms: 1905–29', *Quarterly Journal of Economics*, **99**, 523–46.

Caves, R. and M. Porter (1976), 'Barriers to Exit', in Masson R. and P. Qualls, (eds), *Essays in Industrial Organization in Honour of J. S. Bain*, Ballinger, Cambridge, Mass.

Caves, R. and M. Porter (1977), 'From Entry Barriers to Mobility Barriers: Conjectural Decisions and Contrived Deterrence to New Competition', *Quarterly Journal of Economics*, **97**, 247–21.

Caves, R. and M. Porter (1978), 'Market Structure, Oligopoly, and Stability of Market Shares', *Journal of Industrial Economics*, **26**, 189–313.

Caves, R. and M. Porter (1980), 'The Dynamics of Changing Seller Concentration', *Journal of Industrial Economics*, **19**, 1–15.

Clarke, D. (1976), 'Econometric Measurement of the Duration of Advertising Effects on Sales', *Journal of Marketing Research*, **13**, 345–57.

Comanor, W. (1964), 'Research and Competitive Product Differentiation in the Pharmaceutical Industry', *Economica*, **81**, 372–84.

Comanor, W. (1966), 'Competition and Performance of the Midwestern Coal Industry', *Journal of Industrial Economics*, **14**, 211–25.

Comanor, W. and T. Wilson (1967), 'Advertising, Market Structure and Performance', *Review of Economics and Statistics*, **49**, 423–40.

Comanor, W. and T. Wilson (1974), *Advertising and Market Power*, Harvard University Press, Cambridge, Mass.

Comanor, W. and T. Wilson (1979), 'Advertising and Competition: A Survey', *Journal of Economic Literature*, **17**, 453–76.

Connolly, R. and S. Schwartz (1985), 'The Intertemporal Behaviour of Economic Profits', *International Journal of Industrial Organization*, **3**, 465–72.

Cowling, K., J . Cable, M. Kelly and T. McGuinness (1975), *Advertising and Economic Behaviour*, Macmillan, London.

Cubbin, J. (1981), 'Advertising and the Theory of Entry Barriers', *Economica*, **48**, 289–98.

Cubbin, J. and S. Domberger (1988), 'Advertising and Post-Entry Oligopoly Behaviour', *Journal of Industrial Economics*, **37**, 123–40.

Cubbin, J. and P. A. Geroski (1987), 'The Convergence of Profits in the Long Run: Interfirm and Interindustry Comparisons', *Journal of Industrial Economics*, **35**, 427–42.

Curry, B. and K. George (1983), 'Industrial Concentration: A Survey', *Journal of Industrial Economics*, **31**, 203–56.

Davies, S. (1980), 'Minimum Efficient Size and Seller Concentration: An Empirical Problem', *Journal of Industrial Economics*, **28**, 287–302.

Demsetz, H. (1979), 'Accounting for Advertising as a Barrier to Entry', *Journal of Business*. **52**. 345–60.

Demsetz, H. (1982), 'Barriers to Entry', *American Economic Review*, **72**, 47-57.
Dixit, A. (1979), 'A Model of Duopoly Suggesting a Theory of Entry Barriers', *Bell Journal of Economics*, **10**, 20-32.
Dixit, A. (1981), 'The Role of Investment in Entry Deterrence', *Economic Journal*, **90**, 95-106.
Dixit, A. and J. Stiglitz (1977), 'Monopolistic Competition and Optimum Product Diversity', *American Economic Review*, **67**, 297-308.
Dixit, A. and C. Shapiro (1985), 'Entry Dynamics with Mixed Strategies', in Thomas, L. (ed) *Strategic Planning*, Lexington Books, Lexington, Mass.
Domberger, S. and Sherr, A. (1987), 'Competition in Conveyancing: An Analysis of Solicitors Charges 1983-85', *Fiscal Studies*, 17-28.
Dorfman, R. and P. Steiner (1954), 'Optimal Advertising and Optimal Quality', *American Economic Review*, **44**, 826-36.
Dorwood, N. (1977), 'Market Structure and Buyer Loyalty', *Journal of Industrial Economics*, **26**, 115-35.
Duetsch, L. (1975), 'Structure, Performance and the Net Rate of Entry into Manufacturing Industry,' *Southern Economic Journal*, **41**, 450-6.
Duetsch, L. (1984), 'Entry and the Extent of Multiplant Operations', *Journal of Industrial Economics*, **32**, 477-89.
Dunne, T. and M. Roberts (1986), 'Measuring Firm Entry, Growth and Exit with Census of Manufacturers' Data', mimeo, Penn State.
Eaton, B. and R. Lipsey (1980), 'Exit Barriers are Entry Barriers: The Durability of Capital as a Barrier to Entry', *Bell Journal of Economics*, **11**, 721-729.
Eaton, B. and R. Lipsey (1981), 'Capital, Commitment and Entry Equilibrium', *Bell Journal of Economics*, **12**, 593-604.
Eaton, B. and R. Ware (1987), 'A Theory of Market Structure with Sequential Entry', *Rand Journal of Economics*, **18**, 1-16.
Eaton, C. and R. Lipsey (1979), 'The Theory of Market Preemption', *Economica*, **46**, 149-58.
Edwards, J., J. Kay and C. Mayer (1987), *The Economic Analysis of Accounting Profitability*, Oxford University Press, Oxford.
Encaoua, D. and A. Jacquemin (1980), 'Degree of Monopoly, Indices of Concentration and Threat of Entry', *International Economic Review*, **31**, 87-105.
Farrell, J. (1986a), 'Moral Hazard as an Entry Barrier', *Rand Journal of Economics*, **17**, 440-449.
Farrell, J. (1986b), 'Communication Between Potential Entrants', GTE Laboratories Working Paper.
Farrell, J. and C. Shapiro (1986), 'Dynamic Competition with Lock-in', UC Berkeley Working Paper.
Ferguson, J. (1974), *Advertising and Competition: Theory, Measurement, Fact*, Ballinger, Cambridge, Mass.
Fisher, F. and J. McGowan (1983), 'On the Misuse of Accounting Rates of Return to Infer Monopoly Profits', *American Economic Review*, **73**, 82-97.
Fisher, F., Z. Griliches and C. Kaysen (1962), 'The Costs of Automobile Model Changes Since 1949', *Journal of Political Economy*, **70**, 433-51.
Flaherty, M. (1980), 'Dynamic Limit Pricing, Barriers to Entry, and Rational Firms', *Journal of Economic Theory*, **23**, 160-182.
Flaherty, M-T. (1983), 'Market Share, Technology Leadership and Competition in International Semi-Conductor Markets', *Research in Technological Innovation Management and Policy*, JAI Press, Greenwich.
Freeman, C. (1963), 'The Plastics Industry: A Comparative Study of Research and Innovation', *National Institute Economic Review*, pp. 22-62.

Fudenberg, D. and J. Tirole (1983), 'Capital as a Commitment: Strategic Investment to Deter Mobility', *Journal of Economic Theory*, **31**, 227-250.

Fudenberg, D. and J. Tirole (1984), 'The Fat-Cat Effect, the Puppy-Dog Ploy, and the Lean and Hungry Look', *American Economic Review*, Papers and Proceedings, **74**, 361-366.

Fudenberg, D. and J. Tirole (1986), 'A Theory of Exit in Duopoly', *Econometrica*, **54**, 943-960.

Fudenberg, D. and J. Tirole (1986), *Dynamics Models of Oligopoly*, Harwood Academic Publishers, New York.

Fudenberg, D., R. Gilbert, J. Stiglitz and J. Tirole (1983), 'Preemption, Leapfrogging and Competition in Patent Races', *European Economic Review*, **22**, 3-31.

Gaskins, D. (1971), 'Dynamic Limit Pricing: Optimal Pricing Under Threat of Entry', *Journal of Economic Theory*, **2**, 306-322.

Gelman, J. and S. Salop (1983), 'Capacity Limitation and Coupon Competition', *Bell Journal of Economics* **14**, 315-325.

Geroski, P. A. (1982), 'Simultaneous Equations Models of the Structure-Performance Paradigm', *European Economic Review*, **19**, 145-58.

Geroski, P. A. (1987), 'Do Dominant Firms Decline?' in Hay, D. and J. Vickers (eds.), *The Economics of Market Dominance*, Basil Blackwell, Oxford.

Geroski, P. A. and A. Jacquemin (1984), 'Dominant Firms and Their Alleged Decline'. *International Journal of Industrial Organization*, **2**, 1-28.

Geroski, P. A. and A. Jacquemin (1988), 'The Persistence of Profits: A European Comparison', *Economic Journal*, **98**, 375-89.

Geroski, P. A. (1988a), 'The Interaction Between Domestic and Foreign Based Entrants', mimeo, London Business School.

Geroski, P. A. (1988b), 'The Effect of Entry on Profit Margins in the Short and Long Run', mimeo, London Business School.

Geroski, P. A. (1983), 'The Empirical Analysis of Entry: A Survey', mimeo, University of Southampton.

Geroski, P. A. and A. Murfin (1987a), 'Entry and Industry Evolution: The UK Car Industry 1958-83', mimeo, London Business School.

Geroski, P. A. and A. Murfin (1987b), 'Entry and Intra-Industry Mobility in the UK Car Market', mimeo, London Business School.

Geroski, P. A. and R. Masson (1987), 'Dynamic Market Models in Industrial Organization', *International Journal of Industrial Organization*, **5**, 1-14.

Geroski, P. A. (1988c), 'Domestic and Foreign Entry in the UK: 1983-1984', mimeo, London Business School.

Ghemawat, P. and B. Nalebuff (1985), 'Exit', *Rand Journal of Economics*, **15**, 184-193.

Ghemawat, P. (1984), 'Capacity Expansion in the Titanium Dioxide Industry', *Journal of Industrial Economics*, **33**, 145-164.

Gilbert, R. (1981), 'Patents, Sleeping Patents, and Entry Deterrence', in S. Salop (ed), *Strategy, Predation and Antitrust Analysis*, Federal Trade Commission Report, Washington, DC.

Gilbert, R. (1989), 'Mobility Barriers and the Value of Incumbency', in R. Schmalensee and R. Willig (eds.), *Handbook of Industrial Organization*, North Holland, New York.

Gilbert, R. (1989), 'The Role of Potential Competition in Industrial Organization', forthcoming, *Journal of Economic Perspectives*.

Gilbert, R. (1986), 'Preemptive Competition', in Stiglitz, J. and F. Mathewson (Eds), *New Developments in the Analysis of Market Structure*, Cambridge, Mass.

Gilbert, R. and R. Harris (1984), 'Competition with Lumpy Investment' *Rand Journal of Economics*, **15**, 197-212.

Gilbert, R. and M. Lieberman (1987), 'Investment and Co-ordination in Oligopolistic Industries', *Rand Journal*, **18**, 17–33.

Gilbert, R. and D. Newbery (1982), 'Preemptive Patenting and the Persistence of Monopoly', *American Economic Review*, **72**, 514–526.

Gilbert, R. and D. Newbery (1984), 'Preemptive Patenting and the Persistence of Monopoly: Comment', *American Economic Review*, **74**, 238–242.

Gilbert, R. and D. Newbery (1988), 'Entry, Acquisition and the Value of Shark Repellent', University of California Working Paper.

Gilbert, R. and C. Matutes (1989), 'Product Line Rivalry with Brand Differentiation', University of California Working Paper.

Gilbert, R. and X. Vives (1986), 'Entry Deterrence and the Free Rider Problem', *Review of Economic Studies*, **53**, 71–83.

Gollop, F. and M. Roberts (1979), 'Firm Interdependence in Oligopolistic Markets', *Journal of Econometrics*, **10**, 313–331.

Gorecki, P. (1986), 'The Impatience of Being First: The Case of Prescription Drugs in Canada', *International Journal of Industrial Organisation*, **4**, 371–96.

Gorecki, P. and J. Baldwin (1987), 'Plant Creation Versus Plant Acquisition: The Entry Process in Canadian Manufacturing', *International Journal of Industrial Organization*, **5**, 27.

Gorecki, P. (1975), 'The Determinants of Entry by New and Diversifying Enterprises in the UK Manufacturing Sector', *Applied Economics*, **7**, 139–47.

Gorecki, P. (1976), 'The Determinants of Entry by Domestic and Foreign Enterprises in Canadian Manufacturing Industries', *Review of Economics and Statistics*, **58**, 495–8.

Gorecki, P. and J. Baldwin (1983), 'Entry and Exit to the Canadian Manufacturing Industry' 1970–79, mimeo, Economic Council of Canada.

Gort, M. (1962), 'Analysis of Stability and Change in Market Shares', *Journal of Political Economy*, **71**, 51–61.

Gort, M. and A. Konakayama (1982), 'Model of Diffusion in the Production of Innovation', *American Economic Review*, **72**, 1111–1120.

Gort, M. and S. Klepper (1982), 'Time Paths in the Diffusion of Product Innovations' *Economic Journal*, **92**, 630–53.

Grabowski, H. and J. Vernon (1982), 'The Pharmaceutical Industry', in Nelson, R. (ed.), *Government and Technical Progress*, Pergamon Press, Oxford.

Haas-Wilson, D. (1986), 'The Effect of Commercial Practice Restrictions: The Case of Optometry', *Journal of Law and Economics*, **29**, 165–186.

Hamilton, R. (1985), 'Interindustry Variation in Gross Entry Rates of 'Independent' and 'Dependent' Businesses', *Applied Economics*, **17**, 271–80.

Harrington, J. (1984), 'Noncooperative Behaviour by a Cartel as an Entry-Deterring Signal', *Rand Journal of Economics*, **15**, 426–434.

Harrington, J. (1986), 'Limit Pricing When the Potential Entrant is Uncertain of Its Cost Function', *Econometrica*, **54**, 429–437.

Harris, C. and J. Vickers (1985), 'Perfect Equilibrium in a Model of a Race', *Review of Economic Studies*, **52**, 193–209.

Harris, M. (1976b), 'Entry and Barriers to Entry', *Industrial Organization Review*, **4**, 165–174.

Harrod, R. (1952), *Economic Essays*, Macmillan, London.

Hause, J. and G. Du Reitz (1984), 'Entry, Industry Growth and the Microdynamics of Industry Supply', *Journal of Political Economy*, **92**, 733–57.

Havrileskiy, T. and R. Barth (1969), 'Tests of Market Share Stability in the Cigarette Industry 1950–66', *Journal of Industrial Economics*, **26**, 193–207.

Hay, D. and D. Morris (1984), *Unquoted Companies*, Macmillan Press, Basingstoke and London.

Hessian, C. (1961), 'The Metal Container Industry', in Adams, W. (ed.), *The Structure of America Industry*, 3rd edition, Macmillian.
Hicks, J. (1954), 'The Process of Imperfect Competition', *Oxford Economic Papers*, pp. 41–54.
Highfield, R. and R. Smiley (1987), 'New Business Starts and Economic Activity', *International Journal of Industrial Organization*, **5**, 51–66.
Hirshey, M. (1981), 'The Effect of Advertising on Industrial Mobility', *Journal of Business*, **54**, 329–39.
Jacquemin, A. (1987), *The New Industrial Organization*, MIT and Oxford University Press.
Jacquemin, A. and Slade, A. (1988), 'Cartels, Collusion and Horizontal Merger', *Handbook of Industrial Organisation*, North-Holland.
Jenny, F. and Weber, A. P. (1978), 'The Determinents of Concentration Trends in the French Manufacturing Sector', *Journal of Industrial Economics*, **26**, 193–207.
Johnston, J. (1960), *Statistical Cost Analysis*, McGraw-Hill, New York.
Joskow, P. and Klenorick, A. (1979), 'A Framework for Analysing Predatory Pricing Policy', *Yale Law Journal*, 213.
Judd, K. (1985), 'Credible Spatial Preemption', *Rand Journal of Economics*, **16**, 153–166.
Judd, K. and B. Petersen (1986), 'Dynamic Limit Pricing and Internal Finance', *Journal of Economic Theory*, **39**, 368–399.
Kamerschen, D. (1968), 'An Empirical Test of Oligopoly Theories', *Journal of Political Economy*, **76**, 615–34.
Kamien, M. and N. Schwartz (1971), 'Limit Pricing and Uncertain Entry', *Econometrica*, **39**, pp. 441–454.
Katz, M. and C. Shapiro (1985), 'Network Externalities, Competition and Compatibility', *American Economic Review*, **75**, 424–440.
Katz, M. (1986), 'Technology Adoption in the Presence of Network Externalities', *Journal of Political Economy*, **94**, 822–841.
Kay, J. and Mayer, C. (1986), 'On the Application of Accounting Rates of Return', *Economic Journal*, **96**, 199–207.
Kessides, I. (1986), 'Advertising Sunk Costs, and Barriers to Entry', *Review of Economics and Statistics*, **68**, 84–95.
Khemani, R. and D. Shapiro (1983), 'Alternative Specifications of Entry Models: Some Tests and Empirical Results', mimeo, Bureau of Competition Policy, Ottawa.
Khemani, R. and D. Shapiro (1985), 'The Determinants of New Plant Entry in Canada', *Applied Economics*, forthcoming.
Klemperer, P. (1986), 'Markets with Consumer Switching Costs', Ph.D. Dissertation, Stanford University.
Kreps, D. and A. M. Spence (1984), 'Modelling the Role of History in Industrial Organization and Competition', in G. Feiwel (ed.), *Contemporary Issues in Modern Microeconomics*, MacMillan, London.
Kreps, D. and R. Wilson (1982), 'Reputation and Imperfect Information', *Journal of Economic Theory*, **27**, 253–279.
Kreps, D. and R. Wilson (1982), 'Sequential Equilibrium', *Econometrica*, **50**, 863–894.
Levin, R. C. (1982), 'The Semi-conductor Industry', in Nelson, R. (ed.), *Government and Technical Progress*, Pergamon Press, Oxford.
Levy, D. (1987), 'The Speed of the Invisible Hand', *International Journal of Industrial Organization*, **5**, 79–92.
Lewis, T. (1983), 'Preemption, Divestiture, and Forward Contracting in a Market Dominated by a Single Firm', *American Economic Review*, **73**, 1092–1101.
Lieberman, M. (1984), 'The Learning Curve and Pricing in the Chemical Processing Industries', *Rand Journal of Economics*, **15**, 213–228.

Lieberman, M. (1987a), 'Post-Entry Investment and Market Structure in the Chemical Processing Industries', *Rand Journal of Economics*, **18**, 533–49.

Lieberman, M. (1987b), 'Excess Capacity as a Barrier to Entry: An Empirical Appraisal', *Journal of Industrial Economics*, **35**, 607–27.

Lyons, B. (1980), 'A New Measure of Minimum Efficient Plant Size in UK Manufacturing Industry', *Economica*, **47**, 19–34.

MacDonald, J. (1986), 'Entry and Exit on the Competitive Fringe', *Southern Economic Journal*, pp. 640–52.

McGuckin, R. (1972), 'Entry, Concentration Change and Stability of Market Shares', *Southern Economic Journal*, **38**, 363–70.

Mankiw, G. and M. Whinston (1986), 'Free Entry and Social Inefficiency', *Rand Journal of Economics*, **17**, 48–58.

Mann, M. (1966), 'Seller Concentration, Barriers to Entry, and Rate of Return in Thirty Industries', *Review of Economics and Statistics*, **48**, 296–307.

Mansfield, E. (1962), 'Entry Gibrats Law, and the Growth of Firms', *American Economic Review*, **52**, 1023–1051.

Mansfield, E., M. Schwartz and S. Wagner (1981), 'Imitation Costs and Potents: An Empirical Study', *Economic Journal*, **91**, 907–18.

Martin, S. (1983), 'Markets, Firms and Economic Performance', *Monograph Series in Finance and Economics*, NYU Graduate School of Business Administration, New York.

Martin, S. (1979), 'Advertising, Concentration and Profitability: the Simultaneity Problem', *Bell Journal of Economics*, **10**, 639–47.

Masson, R. and J. Shaanan (1983), 'Social Costs of Oligopoly and the Value of Competition', *Economic Journal*.

Masson, R. and J. Shaanan (1984), 'Optimal Pricing and Entry Deterrence in Canadian Industry', *International Journal of Industrial Organisation*, **5**, 323–40.

Masson, R. and J. Shaanan (1986), 'Excess Capacity and Limit Pricing: An Empirical Test', *Economica*, **53**, 365–78.

Masson, R. and J. Shaanan (1982), 'Stochastic Dynamic Limit Pricing: An Empirical Test', *Review of Economics and Statistics*, **64**, 413–23.

Masters, S. (1969), 'An Inter Industry Analysis of Wages and Plant Size', *Review of Economics and Statistics*, **54**, 341–45.

Matthews, S. and L. Mirman (1983), 'Equilibrium Limit Pricing: The Effects of Private Information and Stochastic Demand', *Econometrica*, **51**, 981–995.

Matutes, C. and P. Regibeau (1986a), 'Mix and Match: Product Compatibility without Network Externalities', University of California, Berkeley Working Paper.

Matutes, C. and P. Regibeau (1986b), 'Product Compatibility as a Credible Commitment', University of California, Berkeley Working Paper.

McLean, R. and M. Riordan (1989), 'Industry Structure with Sequential Technology Choice', *Journal of Economic Theory*, **47**, 1–21

Meisel, J. (1981), 'Entry, Multiple-Brand Firms and Market Share Instability', *Journal of Industrial Economics*, **29**, 375.

Milgrom, P. and J. Roberts (1982a), 'Limit Pricing and Entry Under Incomplete Information: An Equilibrium Analysis', *Econometrica*, **50**, 443–459.

Milgrom, P. and J. Roberts (1982b), 'Predation, Reputation and Entry Deterrence', *Journal of Economic Theory*, **27**, 280–312.

Mills, D. (1987), 'Preemptive Investment Timing', University of Virginia Working Paper.

Modigliani, F. (1958), 'New Developments on the Oligopoly Front', *Journal of Political Economy*, **66**, 215–232.

Mookherjee, D. and D. Ray (1986), 'Dynamic Price Games with Learning-By-Doing', Working Paper No. 884, Stanford Graduate School of Business.

Morgan, E., I. Lowe and C. Tomkins (1980), 'The UK Financial Leasing Industry: A Structural Analysis', *Journal of Industrial Economics*, **28**, 405–25.
Morrison, S. and C. Winston (1987), 'Empirical Inplications and Tests of the Contestability Hypothesis', *Journal of Law and Economics*, **30**, 53–66.
Mueller, D. (1977), 'The Persistence of Profits Above the Norm', *Economica*, **44**, 369–80.
Mueller, D. (1986), *Profits in the Long Run*, Cambridge University Press, Camrbridge.
Mueller, W. and L. Hamm, (1974), 'Trends in Industrial Concentration', *Review of Economics and Statistics*, **56**, 511–20.
Mueller, W. and R. Rogers (1980), 'The Role of Advertising in Changing Concentration of Manufacturing Industries', *Review of Economics and Statistics*, **62**, 89–96.
Needham, D. (1976), 'Entry Barriers and Non-Price Aspects of Firms Behaviour', *Journal of Industrial Economics*, **25**, 29–43.
Nelson, P. (1970), 'Information and Consumer Behaviour', *Journal of Political Economy*, **78**, 377–329.
Nelson, R. and S. Winter (1982), *An Evolutionary Theory of Economic Change*, Harvard University Press, Cambridge.
Newman, H. (1978), 'Strategic Groups and the Structure-Performance Relationship', *Review of Economics and Statistics*, **60**, 417–427.
O.E.C.D. (1985), *Costs and Benefits of Protection*, Paris.
Ogadiri, H. and H. Yamawaki (1986), 'A Study of Company Profit Rate Time Series: Japan and the US', *International Journal of Industrial Organization*, **4**, 1–24.
Omari, T. and G. Yarrow (1982), 'Product Diversification, Entry Prevention and Limit Pricing', *Bell Journal of Economics*, **13**, 242–248.
Orr, D. (1974a), 'An Index of Entry Barriers and Its Application to the Market Structure Performance Relationship', *Journal of Industrial Economics*, **23**, 39–49.
Orr, D. (1974b), 'The Determinants of Entry: A Study of the Canadian Manufacturing Industries', *Review of Economics and Statistics*, **61**, 58–66.
Parsons, D. and E. Ray (1975), 'The US Steel Consolidation: the Creation of Market Control', *Journal of Law and Economics*, **18**, 181–220.
Peles, Y. (1971), 'Economies of Scale in Advertising, Beer and Cigarettes', *Journal of Business*, **44**, 32–7.
Peltzman, S. (1965), 'Entry in Commercial Banking' *Journal of Law and Economics*, **8**, 11–50.
Perry, M. (1984), 'Scale Economies, Imperfect Competition, and Public Policy', *Journal of Industrial Economics*, **32**, 313–330.
Peters, M. (1984), 'Restrictions on Price Advertising', *Journal of Political Economy*, **92**, 472–485.
Porter, M. (1974), 'Consumer Behaviour, Retailer Power, and Market Performance in Consumer Goods Industries', *Review of Economics and Statistics*, **56**, 541–48.
Porter, M. (1976), 'Interbrand Choice, Media Mix, and Market Performance', *American Economic Review*, **66**, 398–406.
Prais, S. (1976), *The Evalution of Gain Firms in Great Britain*, Cambridge University Press, Cambridge.
Prais, S. (1978), 'The Strike Proneness of Large Plants in Britain', *Journal of the Royal Statistical Society*, **A. 141**, 368–84.
Prais, S. (1981), *Productivity and Industrial Structure*, Cambridge University Press, Cambridge.
Pratten, C. (1971), *Economies of Scale in Manufacturing Industry*, Cambridge University Press, Cambridge.
Prescott, E. and M. Visscher (1978), 'Sequential Location among Firms with Perfect Foresight', *Bell Journal of Economics*, **8**, 378–393.

Rees, R. (1973), 'Optimum Plant Size in United Kingdom Industries', *Economica*, **40**, 394–401.
Reinganum, J. (1983), 'Uncertain Innovation and the Persistence of Monopoly', *American Economic Review*, **73**, 741–47.
Reynolds, S. (1986), 'Strategic Capital Investment in the American Aluminum Industry', *Journal of Industrial Economics*, **34** , 225–246.
Richardson, G. (1960), *Information and Investment*, Oxford University Press.
Rogerson, W. (1982), 'A Note on the Incentive for a Monopolist to Decrease Fixed Costs as a Barrier to Entry', *Quarterly Journal of Economics*.
Rosenthal, R. (1981), 'Games of Perfect Information, Predatory Pricing and the Chain Store Paradox', *Journal of Economic Theory*, **25**, 92–100.
Salamon, G. (1985), 'Accounting Rates of Return', *American Economic Review*, **75**, 495–504.
Saloner, G. (1981), 'Dynamic Limit Pricing in an Uncertain Environment', Stanford University Working Paper.
Salop, S. (1979), 'Strategic Entry Deterrence', *American Economic Review*, **69**, 335–338.
Salop, S. and D. Scheffman (1983), 'Raising Rivals' Costs' *American Economic Review*, **73**, 267–271.
Salop, S. and D. Scheffman (1986), 'Cost-Raising Strategies', Federal Trade Commission, Bureau of Economics Working Paper No. 146, July.
Saving, T. (1961), 'Estimation of Optimum Size of Plant by the Survivor Technique' *Quarterly Journal of Economics*, **75**, 596–607.
Schelling, T. (1960), *The Strategy of Conflict*, Cambridge, Harvard University Press.
Scherer, F., A. Beckenstein, E. Kaufer and R. Murphy (1975), *The Economics of Multi-Plant Operation: An International Comparisons Study*, Harvard Press, Cambridge, Mass.
Scherer, F. (1976), 'Industrial Structure, Scale Economies, and Worker Alienation' in R. Masson and P. Qualls (eds.), *Essays in Industrial Organization in Honour of Joe Bain*, Ballinger, Cambridge Mass.
Scherer, F. (1980), *Industrial Market Structure and Economic Performance*, 2nd ed. Rand McNally, Chicago.
Schmalensee, R. (1972), *The Economics of Advertising*, North Holland, Amsterdam.
Schmalensee, R. (1974), 'Brand Loyalty and Barriers to Entry', *Southern Economic Journal*, 579–591.
Schmalensee, R. (1978), 'Entry Deterrence in the Ready-to-Eat Breakfast Cereal Industry', *Bell Journal of Economics*, **9**, 305–327.
Schmalensee, R. (1981), 'Economies of Scale and Barriers to Entry', *Journal of Political Economy*, **89**, 1228–1232.
Schmalensee, R. (1981), 'Product Differentiation Advantages of Pioneering Brands', *American Economic Review*, **72**, 349–365.
Schmalensee, R. (1983), 'Advertising and Entry Deterrence', *Journal of Political Economy*, **90**, 636–653.
Schwalbach, J. (1987), 'Entry into German Industries', *International Journal of Industrial Organization* , **5**, 43–50.
Schwartz, M. (1986), 'The Nature and Scope of Constestability Theory', in D. Morris *et al.* (eds), *Stategic Behavior and Industrial Competition*, Oxford University Press.
Sengupta. J., J. Leonard and J. Vango (1983), 'A Limit Pricing Model for the US Computer Industry', *Applied Economics*, **15**, 297–308.
Shapiro, D. (1983), 'Entry, Exit and the Theory of the Multinational Corporation' in Audretsch, D. and C. Kindleberger (eds.), *The Multinational Corporation in the 1980's*, M.I.T. Press, Cambridge.

Shaw, R. (1974), 'Price Leadership and the Effect of New Entry on the UK Retail Petrol Supply', *Journal of Industrial Economics*, **23**, 65–79.

Shaw, R. (1973), 'Investment and Competition from Boom to Recession: A Case Study in the Processes of Competition — The Dry Cleaning Industry', *Journal of Industrial Economics*, **31**, 69–92.

Shaw, R. (1980), 'New Entry and the Competitive Process in the UK Fertilizer Industry', *Scottish Journal of Political Economy*, **27**, 1–16.

Shaw, R. (1982), 'Product Proliferation in Characteristics Space: the UK Fertilizer Industry', *Journal of Industrial Economics*, **31**, 69–92.

Shaw, R. and S. Shaw (1977), 'Patent Expiry and Competition in Polyester Fibres', *Scottish Journal of Political Economy*, **24**, 117–32.

Shaw, R. and S. Shaw (1983), 'Excess Capacity and Rationalization in the West European Synthetic Fibres Industry', *Journal of Industrial Economics*, **32**, 149–68.

Shaw, R. and D. Simpson (1985), 'The Monopolies Commission and the Process of Competition', *Journal of Industrial Economics*, **6**, 82–96.

Shaw, R. and C. Sutton (1976), *Industry and Competition: Industrial Case Studies*, Macmillan, London.

Selten, R. (1975), 'Reexamination of the Perfectness Concept for Equilibrium Points in Extensive Games', *International Journal of Game Theory*, **4**, 25–55.

Selten, R. (1978), 'The Chain Store Paradox', Theory and Decision, **9**, 127–159.

Shapiro, C. (1983), 'Premiums for High Quality Products as Returns to Reputation', *Quarterly Journal of Economics*.

Shepherd, W. (1967), 'What Does the Survivor Technique Show about Economies of Scale?', *Southern Economic Journal*, **34**, 113–22.

Shepherd, W. (1972), 'The Elements of Market Structure', *Review of Economics and Statistics*, **54**, 25–37.

Sherman, R. and T. Willett (1967), 'Potential Entrants Discourage Entry', *Journal of Political Economy*, **75**, 400–403.

Siegfried, J. and L. Weiss (1974), 'Advertising, Profits and Corporate Taxes Revisited', Review of Economics and Statistics, **56**, 195–200.

Smiley, R. (1988), 'Empirical Evidence on Strategic Entry Deterrence', *International Journal of Industrial Organization*, **6**, 167–80.

Spence, A. M. (1976), 'Product Selection, Fixed Costs, and Monopolistic Competition', *Review of Economic Studies*, **43**, 217–236.

Spence, A. M. (1977), 'Entry, Capacity, Investment and Oligopolistic Pricing', *Bell Journal of Economics*, **8**, 534–544.

Spence, A. M. (1979), 'Investment, Strategy and Growth in a New Market', *Bell Journal of Economics*, **10**, 1–19.

Spence, A. M. (1980), 'Notes on Advertising, Economies of Scale and Entry Barriers', *Quarterly Journal of Economics*.

Spence, A. M. (1981), 'The Learning Curve and Competition', *Bell Journal of Economics*, **12**, 49–70.

Spence, A. M. (1984), 'Cost Reduction, Competition and Industry Performance', *Econometrica*, **52**, 101–122.

Spiller, P. E. and Favaro (1984), 'The Effects of Entry Regulation in Oligopolistic Interaction. The Uruguayan Banking Sector', *Rand Journal of Economics*, **15**, 244–54.

Spital, F. (1983), 'Gaining Market Share Advantage in the Semiconductor Industry by Lead Time in Innovation', *Research on Technological Innovation, Management and Policy*, JAI Press, Greenwich.

Stigler, G. (1958), 'The Economies of Scale', *Journal of Law and Economics*, **1**, 54–71.

Stigler, G. (1965), 'The Dominant Firm and the Inverted Umbrella', *Journal of Law and Economics*, reprinted in his *The Organization of Industry*, Homewood, Ill. R. D. Irwin.

Stigler, G. J. (1968), 'Barriers to Entry, Economies of Scale and Firm Size', Chapter 6, *The Organization of Industry*, Richard D. Irwin, Homewood, Illinois.

Stiglitz, J. (1981), 'Potential Competition May Reduce Welfare', *American Economic Review*, **71**, 184–189.

Stiglitz, J. (1987), 'Technological Change, Sunk Costs and Competition', *Brookings Paper on Economic Activity*, **3**, 883–937.

Stonebraker, R. (1976), 'Corporate Profits and the Risk of Entry', *Review of Economics and Statistics*, **58**, 33–39.

Strickland, A. and L. Weiss (1976), 'Advertising, Concentration and Price-Cost Margins', *Journal of Political Economy*, **84**, 1109–21.

Sylos-Labini, P. (1962), *Oligopoly and Technical Progress*, Cambridge, Mass.

Swann, P. (1970), 'Market Structure and Technological Progress: the Influence of Monopoly on Product Innovation', *Quarterly Journal of Economics*, **89**, 627–638.

Telser, L. (1964), 'Advertising and Competition', *Journal of Political Economy*, **72**, 537–62.

Urban, G., T. Carter, S. Gaskin and Z. Mucha (1984), 'Market Share Rewards to Pioneering Brands', *Management Science*, **32**, 645–659.

Utton, M. (1986), *Profits and Stability of Monopoly*, Cambridge University Press, Cambridge.

Vernon, J. and R. Nourse (1973), Profit Rates and Market Structure of Advertising Intensive Firms', *Journal of Industrial Economics*, **22**, 421–30.

Vives, X. (1982), 'A Note on Sequential Entry', University of California Working Paper.

Waldman, M. (1987), 'Excess Capacity, Limit Pricing and the Free Rider Problem,' *Review of Economic Studies*, **54**, 301–310.

Ware, R. (1984), 'Sunk Cost and Strategic Commitment. A Proposed Three-Stage Equilibrium', *Economic Journal*, **94**, 370–378.

Waterson, M. (1984), *Economic Theory of the Industry*, Cambridge University Press, Cambridge.

Weiss, L. (1964), 'The Survivor Technique and the Extent of Sub-optimal Capacity', *Journal of Political Economy*, **72**, 246–61.

Weiss, L. (1969), 'Advertising, Profits and Corporate Taxes', *Review of Economics and Statistics*, **51**, 421–30.

West, D. (1981), 'Testing for Market Pre-emption Using Sequential Location Data', *Bell Journal of Economics*, **12**, 129–143.

White, L. (1977), *The Automobile Industry Since 1945*, Harvard University Press, Cambridge, Mass.

Weitzman, M. (1983), 'Constestable Markets: An Uprising in the Theory of Industry Structure: Comment', *American Economic Review*, **73**, 486–487.

Weizsacker, C. von (1980), 'A Welfare Analysis of Barriers to Entry', *Bell Journal of Economics*, **11**, 399–420.

Williamson, O. (1963), 'Selling Expense as a Barrier to Entry', *Quarterly Journal of Economics*, **77**, 112–128.

Williamson, O. (1968), 'Wage Rates as Barriers to Entry: The Pennington Case in Perspective', *Quarterly Journal of Economics*, **85**, 85–116.

Williamson, O. (1975), *Markets and Hierarchies: Analysis and Antitrust Implications*, The Free Press, New York.

Williamson, O. (1985), *The Economic Institutions of Capitalism*, The Free Press, New York.

Wright, N. (1978), 'Product Differentiation, Concentration and Changes in Concentration', *Review of Economics and Statistics*, **60**, 628–31.

Yip, G. (1982), *Barriers to Entry: A Corporate-Strategy Perspective*, Lexington Books, Lexington, Mass.

Brown Shoe Co., Inc v United States, 370 US 294 (1962).
Telex Corp. v. International Business Machines Corp., 510 F.2d 894 (1975).
US v. Aluminum Company of America, 148 F.2d 416 (1945).

INDEX

INDEX